Field Guide

to

ALASKAN

WILDFLOWERS

A

Roadside

Guide

Alaskan Summers
Cast Their Spell,
On Those With
Strength and Power,
To Explore The Vast Horizons,
And The Tiny Mountain Flowers.
V.E.P.

NOTE TO THE READER

Information on the edibility of wild plants has been included in this book merely as points of interest to the reader, and/or use in field survival situations. The identification and processing of any wild plant for use as food requires reasonable caution and attention to detail since, as indicated in the text, certain parts of some plants are totally unsuitable for use and, in some instances, are even lethal. Personal allergies or sensitivities may also be cause for adverse reactions. Because attempts to use any wild plants for food depend on various factors controlled only by the reader, neither the author nor the publisher assumes any responsibility for such adverse health effects as might be encountered in the individual case.

It is illegal in many areas to pick or dig plants and, in the interest of conservation, it is recommended that you do not gather plants in the wild. Now that Wildflower Gardening has become so popular, many gardeners and nurseries are offering seeds and transplants for sale. If you do choose to garden with wildflowers, please always remember that no plants take care of themselves. When in a garden environment, wildflowers require as much care as any other plants.

Near the Hot Springs, just north of Atlin, British Columbia, Canada
Monkey Flower

Field Guide to

Alaskan Wildflowers

Worthington Glacier, Mile 29.4, Richardson Highway
Fireweed and Sitka Burnet

Verna E. Pratt

Alaskakrafts, Inc.
7446 East 20th Avenue
Anchorage, AK 99504-3429

Thirteenth Printing-2004

Library of Congress Catalog Card Number.......89-84536

ISBN 0-9623192-0-1

Printed in Korea by Samhwa Printing Co., Ltd.

All photographs are by Verna and Frank Pratt, unless otherwise credited.

Illustrations by Verna E. Pratt.

General Editor---Frank G. Pratt

Technical Editor---Verna E. Pratt

Technical Stuff: (for those who bother to read the fine print)

The camera-ready copy for this volume was produced using Pagemaker software on a
home-built 386 computer and a Laserjet IIP printer. Photographic equipment by Canon,
Nikon, and Hasselblad. Films used were Kodachrome, Ektachrome and Fujichrome.
Pagemaker ©---Aldus Corporation, Seattle, WA.
Laserjet©---Hewlett-Packard Company, Palo Alto, CA
Canon ©---Canon Inc., Tokyo, Japan
Nikon ©---Nippon Kogaku K. K., Tokyo, Japan
Hasselblad ©---Victor Hasselblad Aktiebolag, Göteborg, Sweden
Ektachrome & Kodachrome ©---Eastman Kodak, Rochester, NY
Fujichrome ©---Fuji Film, Tokyo, Japan

Cover Photo: Salmonberry Flower,
Summit Lake, Thompson Pass, Richardson Hwy.

DEDICATED

To my mother, Ruth Goldthwaite. It was she who, during my childhood and adolescent years in Massachusetts, instilled in me the love of flowers and nature, through gardening and nature walks.

Forget-me-nots, Mouse-ear Chickweeds, Shooting Stars, and Aleutian Speedwell in Wildflower Garden in front of the author's home in Anchorage.

As you wander through the woodlands,
Bogs, meadows and the fields,
Into your view springs the beauty,
That only Nature yields.

V.E.P.

ACKNOWLEDGEMENTS

My thanks to all my friends who; after accompanying me across bogs and streams, through dense alder thickets, and up the sides of mountains; have still encouraged me to proceed with the writing of this book.

Special thanks to:

Aline Strutz, a long-time Anchorage resident and botanist, who inspired me to pursue learning all I could about the native plants.

Dr. Marilyn Barker, Instructor of Botany, University of Alaska at Anchorage, who assisted in proofreading.

Lynn and Mark Catlin of Anchorage who assisted in proofreading.

And, last, but not least, my husband, Frank, who patiently stopped so many times along the highways, climbed so many mountains, and forded so many streams in search of yet another elusive flower to photograph. Without his diligent efforts in computerizing all the information between these covers, the publication of this volume would have been impossible.

Verna E. Pratt

Table of Contents

INTRODUCTION

This book was written, **and arranged by color**, with the amateur botanist in mind. Through my own experience in learning the wildflowers of Alaska, and through teaching classes on Wildflower Identification in the Anchorage Community Schools program, I have discovered this system to be the most useful to the average person. Color is the first characteristic that we notice when looking at a plant. Placement of plants in this book was difficult in some instances because of color variances, which have been noted.

I feel it is imperative that observation of other plant characteristics also be taken into consideration, so I have stressed these items important to identification. The plants pictured are seen along major highways and at pull-offs and campsites along the way.

This is by no means a complete guide to all of Alaska's flowers, as there are over 1500 species in the state. You will probably see many species not pictured here, but confusing species and color variations will be mentioned and described where appropriate. Occasionally, flowers will have an uncommon number of petals for the variety. Other specifics, such as, toxicity, edibility and economic uses of some plants will be mentioned. Alaska's climactic changes sometimes cause plants to be as much as two weeks ahead or behind the normal blooming times. The amount of snowfall, severity of winter, timing of snow meltoff, etc. are controlling factors. Alaska is the largest of the 50 states, with an area of some 586,400 square miles. Elevations range from sea level to the 20,320 foot heights of the spectacular Mt. McKinley (Denali), the highest peak in North America. This combination of large area and great variation in elevation causes very diverse growing conditions and seasons. Plants that grow in the alpine will be much smaller than the same species at lower elevations. Severe weather, wind, and shallow soil cause plants to hug the ground. Alpine conditions occur at lower elevations in Alaska than in the Rockies. For instance, plants found growing at 8000 to 10000 foot elevation in Colorado might be found at 3000 to 5000 feet in Southcentral Alaska and at only 100 to 500 feet above sea level in the Arctic Coastal areas.

There are now many introduced species---often called weeds, that have become established along the roadways and near farmlands. Among these are Clovers, Sweet Clovers, and Mustard Weeds. Cover crops which are fast-spreading and many other annual weeds have escaped cultivation in farm areas. Remember "A weed is just a flower out of place". The Alaska Highway Department, in "beautifying" the highways, sows non-native wildflower mixes, including Baby Blue Eyes, annual Baby's Breath, and Iceland Poppy. All of these willingly reseed themselves. Native Alaskan wildflower seeds are not available in bulk for this purpose. Of course, you will see many introduced Dandelions, also. Alaska does have several native dandelions, including a pink (flesh colored) variety, but most are small alpine varieties.

Not all plants mentioned in this volume will be accompanied by photos. It was decided to include photos of the most commonly seen plants, with descriptions and comparisons of confusing species included. Those with photographs will be identified by bold face page numbers in the index. Specific localities or mileposts will be noted if pertinent, or if obvious colonies of plants are present there.

It is my sincere hope that this book will encourage you to look more closely at fine details, and will prove very enjoyable and useful to you in your explorations in the plant world.

Verna E. Pratt

Anchorage, Alaska
March 1990

Page viii

BLUE & VIOLET-FLOWERED PLANTS

Coastal Meadow, Kodiak Island
Wild Geranium, Chocolate Lily, Sitka Valerian, False Hellebore, Coastal Paintbrush

Wild Blue Flax (Chitina)

WILD BLUE FLAX

Linum perenne

Family: Flax / Linaceae

Habitat: Very dry, sandy soil at lower elevations in eastern and central Alaska.

Blooming Time: Late June and July.

Description: A wispy plant (15 to 20" tall) with narrow, glabrous, blue-green leaves. The 1" blue flowers have 5 rounded, overlapping petals and 5 stamens.

Comments: The fibers of this plant have been used to weave into yard goods (linens), and it is a source for Linseed Oil.

Purple Cress (Eagle Summit)

PURPLE CRESS

Cardamine purpurea

Family: Mustard / Brassicaceae

Habitat: Wet tundra and meadows in central and western Alaska.

Blooming Time: Late May and June.

Description: A small (2 to 4" tall), showy plant with clusters of small 4-petaled flowers. Colors range from white to pink, lavender and purple. The glabrous, dark green leaves are pinnately divided with narrow leaflets near the base and a broad leaflet at the end.

Comments: Leaves make a tasty addition to a salad.

WILD IRIS OR BLUE FLAG

Iris setosa

Family: Iris / Iridaceae

Habitat: Bogs, meadows and shores of lakes and streams throughout most of Alaska, except northeastern and north of the Brooks Range.

Blooming Time: June and July.

Description: A plant, 12 to 24" tall, with broad, thin, swordlike leaves and a thick, round flower stalk. Flowers have 3 large, purple, blue or violet-colored (rarely white) falls (petal-like sepals) and 3 narrow, upright petals. The seed pod is large and divided into 3 sections. This is a large, showy flower, from 2-1/2 to 4" across.

Comments: A poisonous plant, causing vomiting. Individuals using edible plants should be careful not to confuse Wild Iris with edible cattail which also has long, narrow leaves and grows in standing water.

Wild Iris (Turnagain Pass)

BLUEBELLS, LUNGWORT, LANGUID LADY, CHIMING BELLS

Mertensia paniculata

Family: Borage / Boraginaceae

Habitat: Woods and meadows throughout most of Alaska except Southeastern and north of the Brooks Range.

Blooming Time: June and July.

Description: A plant with many stems, 18 to 30" tall, with hairy, dark green leaves that are broad at the base and tapering to a long point. The flowers are tubular (funnel-shaped), pink in bud, later turning blue; occasionally all pink.

Comments: This is an edible plant though somewhat fishy tasting. A related species, Oyster Leaf, *Mertensia maritima*, is a coastal plant found growing on beaches. It has very small blue, or sometimes white, flowers and thick succulent, fairly broad leaves that are frequently a light bluish-green color.

Bluebells (Eklutna)   Marilyn Barker

Tall Jacob's Ladder (Kenai Peninsula)

TALL JACOB'S LADDER

Polemonium acutiflorum

Family: Phlox, Polemonium / Polemoniaceae

Habitat: Fields, wet meadows and near streams throughout most of Alaska, except Southeastern.

Blooming Time: July and August.

Description: A tall perennial plant, 10 to 36", with sticky, hairy stems. Leaves are smooth and have 7 to 11 sharply pointed leaflets. Flowers have 5 sharply pointed violet-blue petals joined at the base with white centers and hairy, sticky sepals.

Comments: A very variable plant due to habitat and elevation.

BEAUTIFUL JACOB'S LADDER

Polemonium pulcherrimum

Family: Phlox, Polemonium / Polemoniaceae

Habitat: Dry, rocky areas, fields and roadsides, in Southeastern, Southcentral, eastern Central Alaska and the Aleutian Chain.

Blooming Time: Late May to late June.

Description: A low perennial plant, 8 to 14", with many flowers on branched stems. Leaves have 10 to 15 rounded leaflets. The flowers are joined at the base and have 5 rounded violet-blue petals that are white at the base and have yellow centers.

Comments: Northern Jacob's Ladder, *Polemonium boreale,* is a less common alpine variety with sticky, hairy stems.

Beautiful Jacob's Ladder (Copper Center)

PASQUE FLOWER, SPRING CROCUS

Pulsatilla patens

Family: Buttercup, Crowfoot / Ranunculaceae

Habitat: Dry or sandy soil in Interior Alaska.

Blooming Time: May to very early June.

Description: A very silky, hairy plant that is quite varied throughout the season. Spring version is covered with silky hairs topped by a short-stemmed large, cup-shaped flower with 5 to 8 slightly pointed, lavender to violet sepals which are very silky on the underside. As the flower matures, the stem elongates (up to 14") and the flower droops downward. In seed, it is a spectacular sight.

Comments: Seed heads may be picked and dried. Possibly confusing plants are Alaska Blue Anemone, *Anemone multiceps*, which looks like a miniature, dark, bluish-purple Pasque Flower; and, *Anemone Drummondii* whose flowers are more like a miniature Windflower, *Anemone Parviflora* (see White Section).

Pasque Flower in bloom (Bison Gulch)

Pasque Flower seed head (Bison Gulch)

SIBERIAN ASTER

Aster sibiricus

Family: Aster / Asteraceae

Habitat: River flats, meadows, woods, and rocky sub-alpine slopes throughout most of Alaska, except Southeastern.

Blooming Time: July and August.

Description: Stems, 8 to 12" tall, with slightly toothed oblanceolate leaves which are slightly hairy. Flower heads have light lavender ray flowers with yellow centers.

Comments: Might be confused with some Erigerons which have narrower ray flowers and most leaves attached basally. See Coastal Fleabane in Pink Section, page 24.

Siberian Aster (Anchorage)

Mountain Harebell (Chugach Mts.)

MOUNTAIN HAREBELL

Campanula lasiocarpa

Family: Bluebell / Campanulaceae

Habitat: Rocky alpine slopes and ridges throughout most of Alaska.

Blooming Time: July and August.

Description: A very small alpine plant, 2 to 4", with small, oblong, toothed leaves at base becoming narrow up the stem.

Flowers are violet-blue, upright bells, usually singular, and are very large for the size of the plant.

Comments: Similar species is *Campanula uniflora*, with narrow leaves and small flowers.

COMMON HAREBELL, BLUEBELLS OF SCOTLAND

Campanula rotundifolia

Family: Bluebell / Campanulaceae

Habitat: Grassy slopes and rocky outcroppings mostly at lower to mid elevations in Southeastern, Coastal Southcentral Alaska, Kodiak Island; and, occasionally inland.

Blooming Time: July and August.

Description: A slender plant, 8 to 14", with many flowers, having almost heart-shaped basal leaves. The stem leaves are long and narrow and dark-green colored. The flowers are large, violet-blue bells, usually nodding.

Comments: A common plant seen hanging on rocky cliffs near the coast. Seed capsules are interesting dried specimens. A similar species is, *Campanula aurita*, which grows in eastern Interior Alaska in similar locations and has broader stem leaves. Its narrow tubular petals open to dark blue 1" stars.

Common Harebell (Turnagain Arm)

MONKSHOOD

Aconitum delphinifolium, ssp. delphinifolium

Family: Buttercup or Crowfoot/ Ranunculaceae

Habitat: Woodlands, meadows, into mid-alpine areas over most of Alaska.

Blooming Time: July and August.

Description: A tall slender plant, 2 to 4', (much smaller in alpine areas). Leaves usually have 5 deeply-divided, narrow lobes which are divided again, usually into 3 linear segments. Flowers which are scattered on a long stem above the leaves are shaped like a helmet and range in color from light blue to navy blue; and, occasionally, white.

Comments: *Ssp. Chamissonianum* is a more leafy, taller, many-flowered variety in coastal areas. **A poisonous plant, DO NOT EAT.** Once called wolfbane, as it was used in bait for killing wolves. Can be dried for use in decorative arrangements by hanging upside-down.

Monkshood (Anchorage)

LARKSPUR

Delphinium glaucum

Family: Buttercup or Crowfoot/ Ranunculaceae

Habitat: Moist meadows and woodlands throughout Southcentral, Interior and most of interior Southwestern Alaska.

Blooming Time: July and August.

Description: A very tall, 4 to 6', robust plant with many broad, deeply divided, 5-lobed leaves that are again divided into several sections. The main stem, which is frequently purplish, is topped by many purplish-blue, 5-petaled, spurred flowers.

Comments: A poisonous plant. DO NOT EAT. Can be dried for use in decorative arrangements by hanging upside-down.

Larkspur (Chugach Mts.)

Alaska Violet (Chugach Mts.)

Marsh Violet (Anchorage)

Dog Violet (Turnagain Arm)

ALASKA VIOLET

Viola Langsdorfii
Family: Violet / Violaceae
Habitat: Alpine meadows and along streams in coastal areas throughout Southeastern, Southcentral, Southwestern Alaska and the Aleutian Chain.
Blooming Time: Mid-June and July.
Description: A loose plant with long (up to 8") stems, and heart-shaped leaves with shallow teeth. The 5-petaled, irregular, purple flowers are somewhat square, and have long stems.
Comments: All parts are edible raw or cooked. Flowers may be dipped in sugar syrup and candied as a cake decoration. Other confusing species are: Marsh Violet, *Viola epipsela,* which is found in moist woods, and lake margins throughout Alaska. Dog Violet, *Viola adunca*, which has small, very short stemmed, dark green leaves, and numerous short stemmed purple flowers. It grows in dry, rocky areas and blooms in late May to early June. Selkirk's Violet, *Viola Selkirkii,* which is a more delicate plant with rosy-purple flowers and over-lapping leaf lobes. It grows in moist woodlands and shady slopes.

Other Violets, all early blooming, are:
Wood Violet, *Viola renifolia*, a woodland clump plant with small white flowers. Limited range from Turnagain Arm to Palmer.
Stream Violet, *Viola glabella*, a meadow plant with medium size yellow flowers. Southeastern, coastal Southcentral Alaska and Kodiak Island, see page 27.

Viola biflora, found mainly in alpine meadows in Interior Alaska and western Alaska, has small yellow flowers.

Selkirk's Violet (Turnagain Arm)

ALPINE VERONICA

Veronica Wormskjoldii

Family: Figwort / Scrophulariaceae

Habitat: Meadows and alpine slopes throughout Southeastern, Southcentral and eastern Central Alaska and the Aleutian Chain.

Blooming Time: July and August.

Description: Perennial plant, 5 to 8" tall, with a nonbranching, slightly hairy stem. The slightly toothed, sessile, ovate leaves are mostly opposite on the stem. The small, lavender-blue flowers have 4 petals (the upper one being very broad) and are arranged in a terminal raceme.

Comments: Other varieties frequently seen in wet, lowland areas throughout the southern half of Alaska are *Veronica americana*, Brook Veronica (*Veronica serpyllifolia*), and *Veronica Stelleri*. All have glabrous stems.

Alpine Veronica (Chugach Mts.)

ALPINE FORGET-ME-NOT

Myosotis alpestris, ssp. asiatica

Family: Borage / Boraginaceae

Habitat: Sub-alpine and alpine meadows and slopes (lower in coastal areas) throughout most of Alaska, except Southeastern and the Yukon River drainage.

Blooming Time: Late May-June on south-facing slopes to early August in northern snow beds.

Description: A perennial plant, 6 to 15" tall, with long-stemmed, lanceolate blue-green leaves with many stiff hairs. The plant has 1 or more hairy stems with sessile leaves reducing in size upwards. The flowers are 1/4 to 3/8" across, have 5 rounded blue petals joined at the base with a yellow eye surrounded by white. The spike of flowers is tightly curled in a cyme in bud.

Brook Veronica (Hatcher Pass)

Comments: This is the Alaska State Flower. There are several members of this genus and closely related genera in Alaska. The flower spike is tightly curled in bud. Most have blue flowers, occasionally white or pink. Arctic species belong to the *Eritrichium* genus. They have very short stems, rosettes of small, hairy leaves at the base and the flowers are vivid blue.

Brook Forget-me-not, *Myosotis palustris,* is an introduced robust species with light green, glabrous leaves and pale blue flowers.

Alpine Forget-me-not (Chugach Mts.)

Star Gentian (Chugach Mts.)

Glaucous Gentian (Chugach Mts.)

Four-parted Gentian (Kenai Peninsula)

STAR GENTIAN

Swertia perennis

Family: Gentian / Gentianaceae

Habitat: Moist woods and sub-alpine meadows in Southeastern, Southcentral, southern Interior Alaska, and the Aleutian Chain.

Blooming Time: July and August.

Description: A smooth, stiff plant up to 15" tall, often with a purplish stem. Leaves are purplish-green, opposite, oval at the base becoming longer and narrower up the stem. The 4 to 5-petaled flowers are purplish and the tube opens into a star shape (salverform).

Comments: Confusing species, Marsh Felswort, *Lomatogonium rotatum,* has light blue flowers, very narrow leaves, and grows in wet, marshy areas at low elevations. *Gentiana barbata* is a tall (12 to 18") frail specimen with very dark blue, 4-petaled flowers. It is found in dry, open fields in Interior Alaska and the Yukon Territory. Most members of the Gentian family have rigid stems and stiff opposite, smooth, untoothed leaves.

GLAUCOUS GENTIAN

Gentiana glauca

Family: Gentian / Gentianaceae

Habitat: Sub-alpine and alpine slopes and on the tundra throughout most of Alaska.

Blooming Time: July and August.

Description: A small, stiff plant, 2 to 6" tall, with a tight basal rosette of round, yellowish-green leaves. Flowers are a tube of dark blue or bluish-green connected petals which open with a slight flare in sunshine.

Comments: There are many Gentians in Alaska including Four-parted Gentian, *Gentiana propinqua,* a spindly plant, which has violet to pinkish tubular (salverform) 4 to 5-petaled flowers that blooms in mid-summer. It is common fo fields and woodlands. *Gentiana platypetala* (an alpine meadow variety) with very large, sky-blue flowers that bloom during August and September.

ARCTIC LUPINE

Lupinus arcticus

Family: Pea / Fabaceae

Habitat: Dry slopes, fields, and roadsides throughout most of Alaska, except southern coastal areas.

Blooming Time: June and early July.

Description: A perennial plant (10 to 16" tall) with many large, full flower stalks. The distinctive palmate leaves consisting of several oval, pointed leaflets and have long stems. The stout flower stalks look wooly in bud due to the hairy calyx lobes. The flowers are blue to dark-blue and very showy.

Comments: A similar, taller (15 to 36") species which grows in Southeastern, Southcentral, and the Aleutian Chain is Nootka Lupine, *Lupinus nootkatensis*. Its leaves are more blunt, have shorter stems, and numerous flower stalks. The pea-shaped seed pods are covered with small hairs. **Lupines are very poisonous plants, especially the seeds. DO NOT EAT.**

BLACKISH OXYTROPE, PURPLE OXYTROPE

Oxytropis nigrescens

Family: Pea / Fabaceae

Habitat: Exposed, dry, rocky alpine areas throughout most of Alaska, except Southeastern and the Aleutian Chain.

Blooming Time: Late May to late June.

Description: A very low, sprawling plant with a deep tap root and grayish-green leaves with 9 to 13 small pointed leaflets. The flowers are purple, usually in pairs, and the calyx is covered with small black hairs. Seed pods are large, lie on the tundra, and are also covered with black hairs.

Comments: Similar *Astragalus* species usually have more rounded, darker green, nearly hairless leaves and white, lavender or bluish flowers

Arctic Lupine (Glenn Hwy.)

Nootka Lupine (Chugach Mts.)

Blackish or Purple Oxytrope (Sheep Mt.)   Marilyn Barker

Wild Geranium (Anchorage)

WILD GERANIUM, CRANESBILL

Geranium erianthum

Family: Geranium / Geraniaceae

Habitat: Woodlands and meadows, into alpine areas, throughout Southeastern, Southcentral, and Southwestern Alaska. Also seen in Interior Alaska, but only north to about Delta and Nenana.

Blooming Time: Late June to August.

Description: A tall perennial plant (18 to 30" tall). The large, deeply toothed and palmately divided leaves are slightly hairy and appear coarse. The flowers, which are at the top of the stems, have 5 large, rounded, lavender petals with dark stripes. The long-beaked, 5-parted, seed capsules curl backward releasing the seeds rapidly with considerable force.

Comments: Occasionally seen with white blooms.

FEW-FLOWERED CORYDALIS

Corydalis pauciflora

Family: Earthsmoke / Fumariaceae

Habitat: Very wet alpine meadows throughout most of Alaska.

Blooming Time: Early to late June.

Description: A small, delicate, perennial plant (4 to 8" tall) with watery stems. The bluish-green leaves are mostly basal, deeply divided, and 3-parted; thus, the plant could be mistaken for a Buttercup when not in bloom. The spurred tubular flowers are clustered together at the top of the stems. Color varies from white to rose, blue or lavender. All flowers have a white throat.

Few-flowered Corydalis (Chugach Mts.)

PINK-FLOWERED PLANTS

Open Woods, Alaska Highway, Destruction
Bay, Yukon Territory
Round Leaf Orchid

Common Fireweed (Anchorage)

New shoots of Common Fireweed

Dwarf Fireweed (Kenai Peninsula)

COMMON FIREWEED

Epilobium angustifolium, ssp. angustifolium

Family: Evening Primrose / Onagraceae

Habitat: Meadows and woods throughout most of Alaska.

Blooming Time: July and August.

Description: A tall plant, 2-1/2 to 5 feet, growing from deep horizontal roots. Leaves are lanceolate, and placed alternately on the stem which is usually simple, or occasionally branched. The bright pink flowers have 2 large, rounded petals at the base and 2 slightly smaller rounded petals above. The 4 sepals are long, narrow, pointed and purplish. The lower flowers on the long graceful raceme are 1 to 1-1/2" across and bloom first. Its common name is derived from its ability to revegitate quickly after a fire (due to its deep roots that escape damage). The leaves are bright-colored (orange-red to purplish) in the Fall.

Comments: The flowers are used to make honey and jelly. The leaves are edible, especially the new (red) shoots in the Spring. Inner stems are soft and pithy inside and are very nutritious. Varieties with white or pale pink flowers are sometimes seen. *Epilobium angustifolium ssp. macrophyllum* grows in coastal areas (notably the Kenai peninsula), is considerably taller (up to 7 feet) and has broader (over 1") leaves.

DWARF FIREWEED, RIVER BEAUTY

Epilobium latifolium

Family: Evening Primrose / Onagraceae

Habitat: Along streams or river bars and on scree slopes in the mountains throughout most of Alaska.

Blooming Time: July and August.

Description: Stems somewhat sprawling up to 20" tall. Leaves are lanceolate, alternate on stem, greyish-green, and somewhat fleshy. The 4 sepals are pointed and purplish, and the 4 bright pink petals are ovate and all equal size giving it a very symmetrical appearance. Rarely white or light pink.

Comments: Could be confused with Wild Sweet Pea from a distance when growing on river banks due to similarities in size, color and growth form.

WILLOW HERBS

Epilobium species

Family: Evening Primrose / Onagraceae

Habitat: Damp areas and near streams. Some varieties into alpine, throughout the state.

Blooming Time: Mid-June thru mid-August.

Description: Although they have a stout stalk, many varieties appear spindly due to wide spacing between the leaves. A few have side branches. Height varies from 3 to over 20". All except *Epilobium luteum (*yellow) are white or pink and have small flowers. Petals are indented. Leaves usually oval (somewhat narrower) acute, and sometimes shallowly toothed. Seed head is like Fireweed. Many have withered leaves at the base.

Willow Herb (Anchorage)

PINK PYROLA, WINTERGREEN

Pyrola asarifolia

Family: Wintergreen/Pyrolaceae

Habitat: Moist woodlands and meadows.

Blooming Time: June to early July.

Description: An evergreen plant having a rosette of 1 to 1-1/2", round, soft, thick, shiny leaves and an 8-10" heavy (slightly pinkish) spike of many 5-petaled, slightly nodding, 1/2' pink flowers with distinctive long protruding styles and obvious, rounded, heavy seed capsules.

Comments: *Pyrola minor* is similar but a very small (about 5") alpine plant with 1/4 to 3/8" flowers. *Pyrola grandiflora* is very similar but has slightly larger, more open, white flowers and is found almost exclusively in woods. See page 60, White Section. *Pyrola chlorantha* has very small leaves and small, green flowers. Many of the different species are frequently found growing together. There are 2 varieties of Sidebells Pyrola, *Pyrola secunda*, which have thinner, more pointed leaves and very small, green, bell-shaped flowers that hang to one side of the curved stem. See page 78 in Miscellaneous section.

Pink Pyrola (Anchorage)

Nagoonberry (Anchorage)

Salmonberry (Thompson Pass)

Salmonberry (Mt. Alyeska)

NAGOONBERRY

Rubus arcticus

Family: Rose / Rosaceae

Habitat: Stream banks, moist fields, lake margins, tundra and alpine slopes throughout most of Alaska except the extreme North Slope.

Blooming Time: June and July.

Description: There are 3 varieties in Alaska. These are low plants with long-stemmed, 3-parted, coarsely veined, leaves (much like strawberries) that spread rapidly by underground runners. The 1" flowers have 5-8 long, light pink, narrow petals. In late July or August they bear small, red, very tasty (raspberry-like) berries, but, generally do not produce well except in Southeastern Alaska.

Comments: Similar species are: Trailing Raspberry, *Rubus pedatus*, having a similar berry, 5-petaled white flowers but having 5 leaflets, and found trailing along the ground in very moist woodlands and some alpine areas in Southeastern and Southcentral Alaska. Berries ripen late in the season. Salmonberry, *Rubus spectabilis*, has a flower similar to Nagoonberry with 5 larger, broader bright pink petals. The tasty, but seedy, long (blackberry-like) berry ripens in late July and August and may be yellow, orange or red. They are a favorite food of bears. The 3 to 5 foot tall, shrubby biennial canes, which may have a few prickles, form dense thickets in moist coastal and mountainous areas in Southeastern and Southcentral Alaska. (See Cloudberry, *Rubus chamaemorus* on page 67 in White section).

Salmonberry leaf

PRICKLY ROSE

Rosa acicularis

Family: Rose / Rosaceae

Habitat: Open woods, clearings, meadows throughout most of Alaska, except the North Slope and Southeastern.

Blooming Time: June to early July.

Description: A very prickly shrub, 1-1/2 to 6' tall, generally with toothed 5-parted compound leaves with distinct stipules. The large, showy flowers (2 to 3") have 5 rounded (sometimes notched) pink, soft, velvet-like petals. Twigs are very red in the Winter and the leaves turn reddish in the Fall.

Prickly Rose (Anchorage)

Comments: Similar species Nootka Rose, *Rosa nutkatensis*, has only a few spines and usually a more rounded hip. It is found in Southeastern Alaska, Kodiak Island, the Kenai Peninsula, and Turnagain Arm. These species frequently hybridize when their zones overlap. The petals are used to make jelly or tea and the "hip" or fruit, which is orange to red, is used for jellies, jams, teas and in baked goods; and is very high in Vitamin C. Do not eat the seeds as they have 2 prongs that might lodge in your intestines and cause considerable problems.

Rose "hips" (Anchorage)

SPRING BEAUTY

Claytonia sarmentosa

Family: Purslane / Portulacaceae

Habitat: Wet, rocky alpine slopes, near streams and snow beds throughout most of Alaska, except Southeastern and the extreme North Slope.

Blooming Time: July and August.

Description: A small, delicate, fleshy plant with small spatulate, edible, light greenish-yellow leaves and small (3/4"), 5-petaled, white to light pink flowers with darker veins and 2 deciduous sepals.

Comments: There are several Spring Beauties in Alaska. Most have showy, pink to white flowers and are small plants, except Siberian Spring Beauty, *Claytonia sibirica*, which is found in moist areas at low elevation in Southeastern Alaska, southern coastal areas, and the Aleutian chain. It is 12 to 20" tall with many, very small, pink or white flowers. Spring Beauty makes a nice addition to salads. *Claytonia sibirica* tastes similar to beet greens.

Spring Beauty (Thompson Pass)

Shooting Star (Anchorage)

Frigid Shooting Star (Denali Hwy.)

SHOOTING STAR

Dodecatheon pulchellum

Family: Primrose / Primulaceae

Habitat: Wet coastal meadows in Southeastern and Southcentral Alaska.

Blooming Time: June

Description: Perennial plant with smooth oblanceolate basal leaves. The flowering stalk is leafless and 10-15" tall with many flowers that have 5 reflexed, bright pink petals with a yellow ring at the base. Seed capsules are cylindrical and rust colored.

Comments: Subspecies *Alaskanum* is a shorter plant of coastal areas. *Dodecatheon pauciflorum* is a tall plant in the Tok area with few flowers. *Dodecatheon Jeffreyii*, found in Southeastern and coastal areas, generally does not have the yellow ring visible. The only other plant in Alaska with similar flowers is Bog Cranberry, *Oxycoccus microcarpus*, which is a very small, trailing evergreen shrub with very tiny, light pink flowers, found in bogs. See drawing on page 69 in Pink Section.

FRIGID SHOOTING STAR

Dodecatheon frigidum

Family: Primrose / Primulaceae

Habitat: Wet alpine meadows and tundra throughout most of Alaska, except Southeastern and South-central coastal areas.

Blooming Time: Mid-June to late-July.

Description: A smaller plant (up to 8") with petiolate, spade-shaped, slightly dentate leaves (1 to 2-1/2" long). Flowers are usually magenta, have 5 reflexed petals, but seldom show any yellow.

MOSS CAMPION

Silene acaulis
Family: Pink / Caryophyllaceae
Habitat: Dry, rocky alpine areas.
Blooming Time: June and July.
Description: A low "cushion" plant forming tight "moss-like" mats of narrow, short, flat leaves. They are covered with small (1/2"), light pink, very aromatic (like lilac), 5-petaled, salverform flowers.
Comments: A confusing species is *Douglasia Gormanii* (Primrose family), a smaller, looser plant with small, 5-petaled, bright pink flowers, found in rocky alpine areas of Interior

Moss Campion (Chugach Mts.)

Alaska. Primrose flowers have only 5 stamens which are located over the midlines of the petals, while Pink family flowers have 10 stamens (see Plant Families section).

TWIN FLOWER

Linnaea borealis

Family: Honeysuckle / Caprifoliaceae

Habitat: Woods and dry slopes in the mountains throughout most of Alaska.

Blooming Time: Mid-June to early August.

Description: A trailing shrub with small, rounded, light green, evergreen leaves placed opposite on the stems, and having a few teeth near the tip. The flowering stems have 1 to 2 sets of leaves and usually 2 pinkish-white, bell-shaped flowers, borne on 3 to 4" stems.

Twin Flower (Anchorage)

BOG ROSEMARY

Andromeda polifolia

Family: Heath / Ericaceae

Habitat: Bogs and moist depressions in the mountains throughout most of Alaska.

Blooming Time: Late May thru June.

Description: Dwarf evergreen shrub, up to 8" tall, having thick, long, narrow leaves that are grayish-green above and silvery-white beneath with edges rolled under. The light pink, urn-shaped flowers are clustered at the end of the branches. The flower stems are also pink.

Comments: This is a very poisonous plant causing rapid lowering of blood pressure if eaten. DO NOT EAT.

Bog Rosemary (Anchorage)

Fairy Slipper (King Mt. Campground)

FAIRY SLIPPER, CALYPSO ORCHID

Calypso bulbosa

Family: Orchid / Orchidaceae

Habitat: Moist, mossy woods in Southeastern, inland Southcentral, and Interior Alaska.

Blooming Time: Mid-May to mid-June.

Description: The 4 to 6" plant is probably semi-parasitic and has a thick, fleshy stem arising from a fleshy bulb with one basal leaf with linear veins. The leaf, which looks pleated, dies after the plant blooms. A new leaf appears in August. There is one pinkish-lavender flower consisting of 3 pointed sepals, 2 pointed petals and a large lower petal which is sac-like. Seen in some roadside areas and pull-offs on the Glenn Highway east of Anchorage in late May.

Comments: A similar larger (8 to 10") species is the Spotted Lady Slipper, *Cypripedium guttatum*, which is cream colored with maroon or brownish flower blotches, and 2 large stem leaves. Lady Slippers are not common in Alaska. A good viewing spot for this orchid is Abercrombie State Park on Kodiak Island, see page 75. The White Lady Slipper, *Cypripedium passerinum*, has 3 to 4 large leaves per stem, is 10 to 12" tall and may be found in mixed woodlands in Interior Alaska, see page 13. Another pink orchid is *Amerorchis rotundifolia* (see page 13, pink section).

PURPLE MOUNTAIN SAXIFRAGE, FRENCH KNOT PLANT

Saxifraga oppositifolia ssp. oppositifolia

Family: Saxifrage / Saxifragaceae

Habitat: Wet, gravelly slopes, ridges and rock crevices in the mountains throughout most of Alaska, except extreme Southeastern (coastal), and the Yukon River Drainage.

Blooming Time: Very early May to early June.

Description: A small, usually loosely matted plant with many tiny, dark green rosettes of leaves (also called French Knot Plant). Flowers are magenta to purple with 5 clawed petals.

Purple Mountain Saxifrage (Bison Gulch)

LAPLAND ROSEBAY

Rhododendron lapponicum

Family: Heath / Ericaceae

Blooming Time: Late May to mid-June.

Habitat: Woods, moist depressions, and alpine slopes in Interior Alaska.

Description: An evergreen shrub, 6 to 18" tall, with small, oval, hard, dark green leaves with rusty undersides, similar to Labrador Tea but leaves appear to be arranged in whorls at the ends of the stems. The

Lapland Rosebay (Bison Gulch)

5-petaled, 5/8" open funnel-shaped, magenta flowers bloom in dense clusters at the end of the branches.

Comments: *Rhododendron camtschaticum*, a very low deciduous shrub with large, 1-1/2" to 2" magenta flowers may be seen in some alpine areas on the Seward Peninsula, Mt. McKinley Park, Kodiak Island, and the Aleutian Chain. See drawing below.

Lapland Rosebay (Bison Gulch)

ALPINE AZALEA

Loiseleuria procumbens

Family: Heath / Ericaceae

Habitat: Acidic, southfacing alpine slopes and ridges throughout most of Alaska.

Blooming Time: Early June.

Description: A dwarf, mat-forming evergreen shrub. Leaves are small, oval and opposite on stems. The clusters of tiny, light pink, 5-petaled flowers make an impressive sight on the top of many mountain slopes. It is frequently found growing with lichen.

Comments: When not in bloom, leaves look similar to Lapland Diapensia, *Diapensia lapponicum,* which has white flowers and grows in the same habitats. See page 73 in White Section.

Alpine Azalea
(Chugach Mts.)

Marilyn Barker

Bog Blueberry (Anchorage)

Bog Blueberry (Chugach Mts.)

Pink Plumes (Denali Hwy.)

BOG BLUEBERRY

Vaccinium uliginosum

Family: Heath / Ericaceae

Habitat: Bogs, woodlands, tundra and alpine slopes throughout most of Alaska.

Blooming Time: Late May and June.

Description: A deciduous shrub up to 2 feet tall (much shorter in alpine areas) with small, 5/8 to 3/4", oval leaves with entire margins. The small, pink, bell-shaped flowers form as the leaves unfurl and produce dark blue, soft, oval to round, tasty, slightly tart berries from July to early September.

Comments: Other varieties are: Dwarf Blueberry, *Vaccinium caespitosum*, which has a sweet, round berry, is very short and found in some alpine areas. Early Blueberry, *Vaccinium ovalifolium*, which is a taller shrub (2 to 3-1/2') with slightly larger leaves, reddish twigs (especially in early Spring). Flowers are white to pink and it has round, firm, blue berries. This shrub is found in moist woodlands and tundra in coastal areas of Southeastern, Southcentral Alaska, and a few areas just south of the Alaska Range. Alaska Blueberry or Huckleberry, *Vaccinium alaskanum*, which is similar to *V. ovalifolium* with black berries and occurs in coastal areas of Southeastern and Southcentral Alaska.

PINK PLUMES

Polygonum bistorta

Family: Buckwheat / Polygonaceae

Habitat: Alpine meadows and heaths throughout most of Alaska, except Southeastern and extreme South Coastal.

Blooming Time: Early June through July.

Description: A plant, 6 to 10" high with long, oval to lanceolate, edible, basal leaves arising from a thick rhizome. The tiny, light pink, flowers are arranged in a dense, long stemmed, spike 1/2 to 3/4" across and 1 to 2" tall.

Comments: Leaves may be eaten raw or cooked.

WOOLY LOUSEWORT

Pedicularis Kanei ssp. Kanei

Family: Figwort / Scrophulariaceae

Habitat: Dry, rocky alpine slopes throughout most of Alaska.

Blooming Time: Late May to mid-June.

Description: Pinnately divided, serrated, petiolate basal leaves surround a thick, wooly flower stalk arising from a long fibrous root. The upper stem leaves are reduced in size. The plant is very short and wooly in bud, elongating in seed (up to 10"). Flowers are many and pink. A very showy plant with 1 to several stalks.

Comments: The common name is derived from olden times when sheepherders thought that the wooly plant harbored lice and infected their sheep. "Wort" means "plant"; thus, "Louse plant". The long root is a good source of starch and is used by the Eskimos. Whorled Lousewort, *Pedicularis verticillata,* is a similar, less densely flowered, pinkish species that has leaves in a whorl around its stems. Arctic Lousewort, *Pedicularis Langsdorfii,* is similar but has lavender flowers. *Pedicularis sudetica ssp. interior* is a taller, darker, variety found in the tundra and also at lower elevations.

Wooly Lousewort (Eagle Summit)

Wooly Lousewort (Eagle Summit)

ELEGANT PAINTBRUSH

Castilleja elegans

Family: Figwort / Scrophulariaceae

Habitat: Rocky alpine slopes of western Interior Alaska and coastal areas of Northern and Northwestern Alaska.

Blooming Time: Mid-June thru July.

Description: A small (4 to 10" tall), branched plant with narrow, pointed, hairy leaves. Lower leaves are entire, but upper leaves are divided. Stems are purplish. Bracts are hairy, light pink to purplish. Flowers are very small and nestled down amongst the colorful bracts.

Comments: *Castilleja Raupii* (of eastern Interior Alaska) is a taller plant with narrow, entire leaves. Bracts are white to pink. *Castilleja parviflora* (of Southeastern Alaska) is a taller plant with many deeply toothed leaves and bright pink bracts.

Elegant Paintbrush (Denali Park)

Coastal Fleabane (Chugach Mts.)

COASTAL FLEABANE

Erigeron peregrinus

Family: Aster / Asteraceae

Habitat: Subalpine and alpine meadows in Southeastern and Southcentral Alaska and the Aleutian Chain.

Blooming Time: July through early September.

Description: A large daisy-type flower with narrow, light pink to lavender, ray flowers. The lanceolate, somewhat hairy leaves are placed alternately on the usually unbranched 6 to 14" stem.

Comments: Siberian Aster, *Aster sibiricus,* a plant of low elevations with numerous lavender ray flowers, and many leaves, is pictured on page 5 in Blue Section. Fringed Fleabane, *Erigeron glabellus,* a similar plant found in Interior Alaska and the Yukon Territory, has less hairy, mostly basal leaves, with narrower ray flowers. There are many small *Erigerons* in Alaska. *Erigerons* have narrow ray flowers. Most are white or pink and grow in gravelly locations, often roadsides.

BEACH PEA

Lathyrus maritimus ssp. maritimus

Family: Pea / Fabaceae

Habitat: Beaches and coastal areas in Southeastern and Southcentral Alaska, Kodiak Island, and scattered areas in Western Alaska.

Blooming Time: Late May to late June.

Description: A sprawling plant, spreading by horizontal roots. The nearly hairless leaves have 6 to 12 oval, slightly pointed leaflets, and tendrils at the ends. Flowers (3/4 to 1" long) are bluish violet and usually occur 4 to 6 on a stem.

Comments: The large pods are eaten, both raw and cooked, by many people. **Caution should be taken with the Pea family as the plants readily absorb selenium from the soil causing toxicity.** Another similar species is Vetchling, *Lathyrus palustris,* a spindly twining plant with long, narrow leaflets and smaller flowers. It is usually found in open woodlands.

Beach Pea (Turnagain Arm)

WILD SWEET PEA

Hedysarum Mackenzii

Family: Pea / Fabaceae

Habitat: Rocky slopes and river bars throughout most of interior Alaska and the North Slope.

Blooming Time: June and July.

Description: A stout, upright plant, 18 to 24" tall, having pinnately divided leaves with 7 to 15 ovate leaflets. The bright pink, very aromatic, pea-shaped flowers are 1/4 to 3/8" wide, and 3/4" long; and are clustered at the top of the stem, making it a short, broad raceme.

Comments: Caution: the root is supposedly poisonous. This plant could be confused with Eskimo Potato which has smaller flowers, longer spikes, and prominent veins on the leaflets. (See Eskimo Potato, below).

Wild Sweet Pea (Glenn Hwy.)

ESKIMO POTATO

Hedysarum alpinum

Family: Pea / Fabaceae

Habitat: Rocky alpine slopes, roadsides and open forests throughout most of Alaska, except Southeastern and the Aleutian chain.

Blooming Time: June and July.

Description: A tall (up to 2 feet, smaller in alpine areas), branched, sprawling plant that grows from a horizontal root. Leaves are pinnately divided with 15-20 ovate leaflets (about 1/2 to 1" long) with obvious mid and branching veins on the under side. Flower stalks are long with many small, light pink to purple, pea-shaped flowers which are up to 1/4" wide and 5/8" long. The flowers usually appear to flow down one side of the stems.

Comments: The root is eaten by the natives, either raw or cooked. Confusing species is Wild Sweet Pea which has mostly smooth underside to leaves, and larger flowers.

Eskimo Potato (Glenn Hwy.)

PARRY'S WALLFLOWER

Parrya nudicaulis ssp. interior

Family: Mustard / Brassicaceae

Habitat: Moist places and sandy slopes in the mountains of the northeastern part of Southcentral Alaska and in Interior Alaska.

Blooming Time: June to July.

Description: Plant with deep rootstalk and long-stemmed, lanceolate basal leaves with a few shallow teeth. The 6-10" flower stalk has several white, pink, or lavender, 4-petalled flowers (about 3/4").

Parry's Wallflower (Eagle Summit)

Comments: This is a very showy plant. There are 2 other subspecies of this plant in western and northern Alaska. Referred to by the Natives as Little Cabbages, the roots and leaves of these plants are used for food, and are very tasty. The aromatic flowers smell like lilacs. See below for leaf differences.

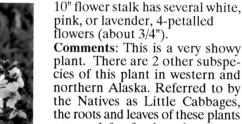

PIXIE EYE PRIMROSE

Primula cuneifolia

Family: Primrose / Primulaceae

Habitat: Rocky alpine areas of Southcentral and western coastal Alaska.

Blooming Time: June and July.

Description: A very small plant with a small rosette of soft, fleshy, light green leaves that are terminally toothed and wedge-shaped at the base. It can be nearly stemless or with flowers on top of a 2-4" stem. The 5-petaled, deeply lobed flowers are usually bright pink, but, occasionally, white. They are tubular at the base and enclosed in a tubular calyx.

Pixie Eye Primrose (Thompson Pass)

Comments: There are several Primroses in Alaska. A few are farinose (having a white powdery substance on the calyx). Most have a rosette of small leaves and a leafless flower stem with 3 to several flowers clustered at the top. Most are white, pink or lavender and have lobed petals. Northern Primrose, *Primula borealis*, is a taller plant with more flowers that is common in Arctic and western coastal areas.

YELLOW-FLOWERED PLANTS

Alpine Meadow, Turnagain Pass
Stream Violet

Alaska Poppy (Denali Hwy.)

Yellow Dryas (King Mt. Campground)

Yellow Dryas seed head (Eklutna)

ALASKA POPPY

Papaver alaskanum

Family: Poppy / Papaveraceae

Habitat: Central Alaska, the Aleutian chain and scattered in some Southcentral areas.

Blooming Time: June and July.

Description: A low (6 to 8") plant with small 5-lobed, slightly hairy basal leaves. Flowers are light yellow, 4-petaled and the seed capsule is almost round. This plant has many of the old dead stems and leaves still attached.

Comments: Other Poppies that might be seen are: *Papaver lapponicum,* a small alpine plant with smaller flowers (sometimes white) and a pear-shaped capsule. *Papaver Macounii,* with larger flowers and is a slightly taller looser plant. *Papaver alboroseum,* a small pale pink poppy. Larger, and in a variety of colors, Iceland Poppy, *Papaver nudicaule*, is seen along roadsides and in waste areas. It has been introduced by the Alaska Highway Department to "reseed with wildflowers". END OF QUOTE! It is NOT native to the area, but has become naturalized.

YELLOW DRYAS

Dryas Drummondii

Family: Rose / Rosaceae

Habitat: Dry gravel areas and river bars throughout interior, southcentral and eastern Alaska.

Blooming Time: June to early July.

Description: A sprawling sub-shrub with oval basal leaves that sometimes have rolled edges. The leaf veins are very prominent and the edges wavy, being greenish-brown above to whitish from hairs underneath. The 2 to 3" high flower stem has no leaves. The calyx has blackish-brown hairs and the flowers are nodding and only partially open. The seed head is in a spiral, opening fully to a tannish fluffy head. It may be seen along the Glenn Highway near the village of Eklutna and is common in gravelly areas near glacial streams.

YELLOW PONDLILY

Nuphar polysepalum

Family: Water Lily / Nymphaeaceae

Habitat: Ponds and slow streams throughout most of Alaska, except western coastal area and north of the Brooks Range.

Blooming Time: July and August

Description: A large plant with small, thin, submerged leaves and large, long-stemmed floating leaves. The large 3 to 4" flowers have 7 to 9 sepals that are green on the underside, and are supported by large, fleshy stems. Petals are very narrow and small.

Comments: This plant has been used as a source of food by many Native groups. The thick root, or rhizome, may be boiled and eaten. The root and seeds may be roasted, ground and used as a grain. The seeds may also be popped like popcorn, and served as a cereal or snack.

Yellow Pond Lily (Kenai Peninsula)

Silverberry (Anchorage)

SILVERBERRY

Elaeagnus commutata

Family: Oleaster / Elaeagnaceae

Habitat: Dry slopes and gravel bars along rivers---especially glacial----in Interior and Eastern Alaska and other scattered locations; such as, Chitina, Glenallen, Circle, and the Matanuska Valley.

Blooming Time: Early to mid-June.

Description: A shrub (3 to 9 feet) with alternate, oblong, slightly pointed, silvery leaves. Both sides of the leaves are rough and scaly like sandpaper. The young twigs are brownish and scaly (older ones dark reddish-brown to black). The yellow, tubular, salviform flowers have 4 silvery sepals turned out flat exposing the yellow interior and 4 stamens. The small, fragrant flowers are in a tight cluster at the base of the leaves. They produce a dry, mealy, scaly, silver berry which is edible but quite tasteless.

Silverberry flower (Anchorage)

Yellow Monkeyflower (Turnagain Pass)

YELLOW MONKEYFLOWER, WILD SNAPDRAGON

Mimulus guttatus

Family: Figwort / Scrophulariaceae

Habitat: Edges of streams, lakes and wet rocky slopes near the coast in Southeastern and Southcentral Alaska and the Aleutian chain. Not too common inland; but, occasionally along rivers in interior Alaska.

Blooming Time: July and August.

Description: A sprawling plant with upright blooming branches that are 8-16" tall. The stem leaves are round to oblong, toothed along the edges, dark green, and opposite. The light green calyx is inflated and holds a 5-petaled irregular-shaped tubed flower with flaring petals (much like a Snapdragon). The petals are bright yellow with reddish spots in the throat. Flowers are large but few.

Comments: The leaves are edible, both raw and cooked. Purple-flowered Monkeyflower, *Mimulus Lewisii*, is in extreme Southeastern Alaska. Yukon Beardtongue, *Penstemon Gormanii* (a vivid violet-blue color) may be seen in the Yukon Territory along the Alaska Highway; and, in Alaska on the Tok Cutoff near Porcupine Creek, and the Steese Highway near Central.

BUTTER AND EGGS, TOADFLAX

Linaria vulgaris

Family: Figwort / Scrophulariaceae

Habitat: Roadsides and waste places. Common around Anchorage, Seward, Palmer and Fairbanks.

Blooming Time: July and August.

Description: An aggressive bluish-green upright plant (10 to 16") with long narrow leaves and spikes of many fairly small (Snapdragon like) flowers that are light yellow and orange and have a very long narrow spur.

Comments: This plant is not native to Alaska, but has become naturalized.

Butter and Eggs (Anchorage)

RATTLEBOX

Rhinanthus minor

Family: Figwort / Scrophulariaceae

Habitat: Open fields and meadows in Southeastern and Southcentral Alaska, the Aleutian chain, and Southwestern coastal Alaska.

Blooming Time: July and August.

Description: An annual plant 12 to 20" tall, usually branched. Leaves are sessile, long and narrow with teeth along the margin. The flowers are small, inconspicuous, and protrude from the calyx. The somewhat hairy calyx forms an urnlike structure that rattles when seeds within the ovary are mature.

Rattlebox (Anchorage)

COASTAL PAINTBRUSH, YELLOW PAINTBRUSH

Castilleja unalaschensis

Family: Figwort / Scrophulariaceae

Habitat: Woods and sub-alpine meadows in southeastern coastal and Southcentral Alaska and the Aleutian chain.

Blooming Time: July and August.

Description: A medium to tall (12 to18") plant with long, pointed, somewhat hairy leaves with 3 to 5 ribs. The flowers are minute and nearly hidden by the yellowish bracts that cluster close to the ends of the stems.

Comments: There are many paintbrushes in Alaska, most of them yellow. Some roadside varieties such as, *Castilleja caudata* and *Castilleja hyperborea* tend to grow in clumps about 12" high. The Elegant Paintbrush, *Castilleja elegans* , is rosy pink, 5 to 10" tall, and grows in Interior Alaska and the North Slope, see page 23 in Pink Section. Red Indian Paintbrush, *Castilleja miniata*, grows in extreme southeastern Alaska. A similar, less reddish, variety,*Castilleja hyetophila,* grows in some other coastal areas.

Coastal Paintbrush (Chugach Mts.)

Capitate Lousewort (Chugach Mts.)

Labrador Lousewort   Marilyn Barker
(Anchorage)

Golden Corydalis (Glenn Hwy.)

CAPITATE LOUSEWORT

Pedicularis capitata

Family: Figwort / Scrophulariaceae

Habitat: Rocky alpine slopes and tundra throughout most of Alaska except South-eastern and Southcentral coastal areas and the Yukon River drainage system.

Blooming Time: June to early July.

Description: A small (3 to 5") plant, with flowering stalk often appearing to be separated from the individual pinnately-divided leaves that are toothed in outline. The few-flowered terminal cluster has large hooded flowers that are pale yellow, the top becoming pink and then rusty in age.

Comments: There are many louseworts in Alaska. Most varieties, except *P. capitata* and some *P. sudeticas* have leaves coming from a main root stalk. There are 4 yellow species in Alaska. Labrador Lousewort, *P. labradorica,* is an annual that grows in bogs, woods and tundra, has many branches and small pale individual flowers. *P. lapponica* is a small, rather inconspicuous, tundra variety found north of the Brooks Range. *P. Oederi* grows in meadows and alpine areas and has a tight spike of many bright yellow flowers.

GOLDEN CORYDALIS

Corydalis aurea

Family: Earthsmoke / Fumariaceae

Habitat: Dry sandy banks, roadsides at low to mid elevations in Interior, Eastern and Southcentral Alaska.

Blooming Time: Late June to mid-July.

Description: An annual or biennial greatly branched, low (3 to 6"), gray-green sprawling plant with pale finely-divided leaves. Flowers are golden yellow, curved and clustered at the ends of branches, later extending as the long curved seed capsules develop.

Comments: An introduced relative, Pale Corydalis or Rock Harlequin, *Corydalis sempervirens*, is a much taller bluish-green plant with pink and yellow flowers and is usually found on disturbed ground.

YELLOW OXYTROPE

Oxytropis Campestris

Family: Pea / Fabaceae

Habitat: Dry stony and sandy slopes from sea level to alpine throughout most of Alaska, except western coastal and the Aleutian Chain.

Blooming Time: Late May and June.

Description: A low Plant (6 to 8") with grayish-green, hairy, pinnately divided leaves with small oval pointed leaflets. The small, light yellow pea-shaped flowers are clustered at the ends of the branches. Old stipules at the base of the plant are light to medium tan in color.

Comments: There are many Oxytropes in Alaska. Other confusing tall species are: *Oxytropis maydelliana* which is similar but has reddish-brown old stipules. *Oxytropis viscida* which has pink or yellowish-white flowers and has slightly sticky leaves. Many Oxytropes contain a toxin and are commonly called Loco-weed, as grazing cattle are strangely affected by it causing an uneven gait. **Do not eat oxytropes.**

Yellow Oxytrope (Turnagain Arm)

HAIRY ARCTIC MILK VETCH

Astragalus umbellatus

Family: Pea / Fabaceae

Habitat: Moist slopes, into alpine, meadows and tundra throughout Eastern and Interior Alaska, the Brooks Range, North Slope, and coastal Western Alaska.

Blooming Time: Mid June to early July.

Description: A low plant (up to 8") with hairy stems and leaves arising from horizontal roots. The leaves consist of several dark green, oval leaflets (often slightly notched at the end). The flower racemes at the ends of the stems have 8 to 12 small, yellow crowded flowers. The calyx is usually covered with dark hairs (occasionally white). The seed pods which look like small peas are also covered with black hairs.

Comments: The edible root is used by some Native people.

Hairy Arctic Milk Vetch (Denali Hwy.)

Eschscholtz Buttercup (Chugach Mts.)

MOUNTAIN BUTTERCUP, ESCHSCHOLTZ BUTTERCUP

Ranunculus Eschscholtzii

Family: Buttercup, Crowfoot / Ranunculaceae

Habitat: Meadows along creeks throughout Southeastern and Southcentral Alaska and the Aleutian chain. Some parts of Interior Alaska.

Blooming Time: Late May and June.

Description: This is a very variable plant in regards to plant and flower size, and shape of leaves. Although not very tall (3 to 6"), it is branched and has many flowers which have 5 shiny rounded petals and 5 yellowish sepals sometimes with yellow hairs. Stems and basal leaves are glabrous and coming from a common root stalk.

Comments: Similar species, Snow Buttercup, *Ranunculus nivalis*, usually has few flowers and leaves and has black hairs on the sepals. **ALL BUTTERCUPS ARE POISONOUS. DO NOT EAT.**

WESTERN BUTTERCUP

Ranunculus Occidentalis

Family: Buttercup or Crowfoot / Ranunculaceae

Habitat: Alpine meadows in Southeastern and Southcentral Alaska.

Blooming Time: June through July.

Description: A plant 8 to 12" tall with 5 somewhat shiny petals, and reflexed sepals. The 3-parted leaves are slightly hairy

Comments: There are many Buttercups in Alaska. Other confusing common short varieties are: *Ranunculus nivalis* (Eastern, Central and Northern Alaska) having sepals with dark hairs, and *Ranunculus Escholtzii* (Southeastern and Southcentral Alaska, and the Aleutian chain) having very shiny petals and shiny leaves. Several tall varieties (12 to 24") may also be seen throughout the state. Most have leaves divided into 3 parts and shiny petals. **ALL BUTTERCUPS ARE POISONOUS. DO NOT EAT.**

Western Buttercup (Kenai Peninsula)

YELLOW ANEMONE, RICHARDSON'S ANEMONE

Anemone Richardsonii

Family: Crowfoot / Ranunculaceae

Habitat: Moist woods near streams and alpine meadows throughout most of Alaska.

Blooming Time: Early June to mid-July.

Description: 4" to 7" tall plant. The basal leaves have long stems, are yellowish-green, 3-parted, notched, and arise from horizontal roots. The flower stem arises from the center of a modified leaf. The flowers have 5 to 8 bright yellow, pointed sepals that are brownish on the underside.

Comments: Often mistaken for Buttercups, but Buttercups have both petals and sepals, the petals are rounded and the stem leaf is positioned to one side of the stem. The leaves of Yellow Anemone and Windflower are similar, except that Windflower has dark veins in the leaves. ALL ANEMONES ARE VERY POISONOUS PLANTS. DO NOT EAT!

Yellow Anemone (Chugach Mts.)

MARSH MARIGOLD

Caltha palustris

Family: Buttercup, Crowfoot / Ranunculaceae

Habitat: Marshes, streams, and margins of lakes in low to mid-elevations.

Blooming Time: Late May to mid-June .

Description: A water plant with hollow stems. Leaves are large (2 to 4"), round to somewhat kidney-shaped or heart-shaped and finely toothed on the edges. Flowers are large (1 to 1-1/2") and have 5 to 7 bright yellow slightly rounded sepals with a greenish cast to the underside.

Comments: This plant is an excellent vegetable when cooked. **It contains a poison when raw**. Mountain Marigold, *Caltha leptosepala*, found in mountain streams, has heart-shaped leaves and white flowers with 5-8 narrow sepals that are bluish on the underside. Blooms very early.

Marsh Marigold (Eklutna Flats)

Shrubby Cinquefoil (Anchorage)

SHRUBBY CINQUEFOIL, TUNDRA ROSE

Potentilla fruiticosa

Family: Rose / Rosaceae

Habitat: Bogs, tundra, and occasionally, alpine slopes throughout most of Alaska.

Blooming Time: Late June, July and August.

Description: A shrub 1-1/2 to 3' tall. The stems are reddish-brown and have shedding bark. The leaves are thick, bluish-gray green above and 5-parted. The flowers are large (1 to 1-1/2") and the petals rounded. A common shrub throughout most of Alaska.

Comments: The only other Potentilla with a similar leaf is *Potentilla biflora*, a plant about 12" tall that grows in high alpine meadows.

Beach Cinquefoil (Eklutna Flats)

BEACH CINQUEFOIL, PACIFIC SILVERWEED

Potentilla Egedii, ssp. grandis

Family: Rose / Rosaceae

Habitat: Seashores, marshes throughout most coastal areas and sometimes along inland rivers and lake edges.

Blooming Time: June and July.

Description: A trailing plant with long runners and long pinnately-divided bright green, smooth leaves. Leaflets are toothed and silvery on the underside. The flowers have 5 petals and many stamens.

Comments: There are 3 other varieties in Alaska, 2 being somewhat smaller plants of northern and western coastal areas, and the other a river variety in Interior Alaska. This is an edible plant, the root being eaten like a potato. *Potentilla anserina* is an introduced variety in waste areas along the Alaska Highway.

ONE-FLOWERED CINQUEFOIL

Potentilla uniflora

Family: Rose / Rosaceae

Habitat: Rocky, exposed slopes and ridges throughout most of Alaska, except Southeastern, the Aleutian Chain and the Yukon River Drainage.

Blooming Time: Mid-May to mid-June.

Description: A low (4 to 8") tufted plant from a stout, course stem with many old dried stipules. The coarsely toothed leaves, which are divided into 3 leaflets, are densely hairy beneath and dark green with a few hairs on the upper surface. The bright yellow flowers (3/4 to 1") have 5 petals with an orange spot at the base, and a slight notch at the end. *Potentilla* petals have a soft velvety look, not shiny like a Buttercup.

Comments: A confusing species is *Potentilla villosa* which is quite common on rocky cliffs of coastal areas. It is 3 to 5" tall with very coarse, leathery looking leaves.

One-flowered Cinquefoil (Chugach Mts.)

SNOW POTENTILLA (CINQUEFOIL)

Potentilla nivea

Family: Rose / Rosaceae

Habitat: Dry open slopes and roadsides in Eastern Alaska, interior portion of Southcentral Alaska, and the Brooks Range.

Blooming Time: Late May to late June.

Description: A small plant (4 to 12") with basal leaves that have 3 distinctly toothed leaflets with tangled wooly hairs on the underside. Stems are branched, leaves are reduced and modified. Flowers are small (1/2 to 3/4") and have 5 petals.

Comments: There are other small-flowered *Potentillas* in Alaska that may hybridize with this species. Hooker's Potentilla, *Potentilla Hookeriana,* is common throughout the Eastern, Central and Southcentral Alaska. It has long hairs on the underside of the leaves.

Many taller varieties of small-flowered *Potentillas* are frequently found introduced along roadsides and growing naturally in some alpine areas. They may have 3 to 7 leaflets. Norwegian Cinquefoil, *Potentilla norvegica*, is commonly seen in fields in July and August. It is 12 to 18" tall, flowers are about 1/2", and leaves have 3 leaflets.

Snow Potentilla (Copper Center)

Norwegian Cinquefoil (Anchorage)

Ross Avens (Chugach Mts.)

ROSS AVENS

Geum Rossii

Family: Rose / Rosaceae

Habitat: Dry stony slopes and snowbeds in Eastern, Central and Southwestern Alaska, the Aleutian chain, and the Brooks Range.

Blooming Time: June and July.

Description: A low plant with dark green pinnately divided compound basal leaves. The 1 to 1-1/4" flowers have 5 rounded petals, large leafy sepals and are clustered at the ends of the 6 to 8" stems which have a few small modified leaves.

Comments: Caltha leaf Avens, *Geum calthifolium,* is a coastal plant found in wet alpine meadows. It has a similar flower, but large round to kidney-shaped leaves that are notched along the margin. Seen in Thompson Pass and Whittier, see drawing below.

LARGE LEAF AVENS

Geum macropyllum ssp. macrophyllum

Family: Rose / Rosaceae

Habitat: Meadows and woods in Southeastern and coastal Southcentral Alaska, and the Aleutian Chain.

Blooming Time: Late June to mid-July.

Description: A tall, erect plant (1-1/2 to 2-1/2') with large pinnately divided leaves. The leaflets are toothed, the terminal one lobed and much larger than the rest. Leaves and stems are covered with stiff hairs. The yellow flowers are small (about 1/2"). The seedhead looks much like a round burr.

Comments: *Ssp. perincisum* is found in Eastern and Central Alaska and has a more deeply divided terminal leaflet.

Large leaf Avens (Kenai Peninsula)

BOG SAXIFRAGE

Saxifraga hirculus

Family: Saxifrage / Saxifragaceae

Habitat: Bogs, meadows and wet tundra throughout most of Alaska, except Southeastern and coastal Southcentral.

Blooming Time: July.

Description: A low, tufted plant that forms small mats of tight, narrow, long leaves. The 3 to 6" stems have short, alternate leaves with 1 to 2 flowers that are 5/8 to 3/4". The flowers have 5 slightly pointed petals with small orange dots near the base and reflexed sepals.

Comments: Spider Saxifrage, *Saxifraga flagellaris*, that grows in rocky alpine areas has a similar flower arising from a rosette of small leaves with red runners that produce new plants.

Bog Saxifrage (Bison Gulch)

YELLOW SPOTTED SAXIFRAGE

Saxifraga bronchialis

Family: Saxifrage / Saxifragaceae

Habitat: Rocky alpine ridges throughout most of Alaska, except extreme south Southeastern and the Yukon River drainage.

Blooming Time: July.

Description: A low tufted plant with very small leaves with fine hairs along the edges. The closely packed leaves form short "sausage-like" stems ending in a nearly leafless 3 to 6" stem with several small (up to 1/2") light yellow flowers with orange dots.

Comments: A similar species is Prickly Saxifrage, *Saxifraga tricuspidata*. See page 59 in White and Cream Section.

Spider Saxifrage (Hatcher Pass)

Yellow Spotted Saxifrage (Chugach Mts.)

Pineapple Weed (Anchorage)

PINEAPPLE WEED

Matricaria matricarioides

Family: Composite / Asteraceae

Habitat: Waste places.

Blooming Time: July and August.

Description: A small, feathery, annual plant (5" to 8") with small yellowish heads that look and smell somewhat like pineapple.

Comments: This is an introduced plant that is commonly seen. The aromatic flower heads can be steeped to make a flavorful tea. They may be used fresh or dried. It is sometimes called Wild Camomile.

COMMON MUSTARD
BALL MUSTARD

Leslia paniculata

Family: Mustard / Brassicaceae

Habitat: Waste places.

Blooming Time: July and August.

Description: An annual plant (1 to 2 feet tall). The light green basal leaves are shaped somewhat like dandelion leaves. Stem leaves are smaller and somewhat arrow shaped. The 4-petaled flowers are very small. The round seeds forming closely behind them.

Comments: This is an introduced plant that has now spread over most of the highly populated areas of the State. The seeds can be ground, added to water and used for mustard seasoning. The leaves are edible, as are most of the mustard family. Another common, introduced variety, is Bird's Rape, *Brassica rapa*, with 1/4 to 1/2" flowers, usually found around farming communities.

Common Mustard (Anchorage)

WHITLOW GRASS

Draba incerta

Family: Mustard, Crucifer / Brassicaceae

Habitat: Dry rocky hillsides, sometimes alpine. Common on the rocks overlooking the Seward Highway south of Anchorage.

Blooming Time: Late May to mid-June.

Description: A small perennial plant with rosettes of small oblong leaves with stellate hairs. Several 4-petaled yellow flowers are clustered at the top on the nearly leafless 2 to 6" stem.

Comments: There are many *Drabas* in Alaska and they are difficult to separate into species. Most are white or yellow and have small rosettes of leaves. *Draba hirta*, *Draba maxima* and *Draba borealis* are all taller, white-flowered varieties that have many stem leaves. *Draba aurea* is a common tall yellow variety.

Whitlow Grass
(Turnagain Arm)

ELEGANT GOLDENROD

Solidago lepida

Family: Daisy, Aster or Composite/Asteraceae

Habitat: Meadows, fields and open woodlands in Southeastern and coastal Southcentral Alaska, and the Aleutian chain.

Blooming Time: July and August.

Description: An erect, leafy plant, 12 to 24" tall. Leaves are pointed, oblanceolate, shallowly toothed, and gradually reducing in size up the stem. Flowers are in a dense terminal raceme of heads.

Elegant Goldenrod (Kenai Peninsula)

Comments: Other species seen are: *Solidago decumbens* (extreme eastern Central Alaska) which is shorter and has smaller spikes, and leaves less toothed. *Solidago Canadensis* (Fairbanks area) which has more loose branched flower heads and entire leaves. Northern Goldenrod, *Solidago multiradiata*, a shorter plant which has very shallowly toothed leaves and dense, more flat flower clusters. It is found throughout the State in rocky woodland and alpine areas.

Northern Goldenrod (Turnagain Arm)

Black-tipped Groundsel (Glenn Hwy.)

Groundsel (Eagle Summit)
Senecio atropurpureus

Triangular-leaved Fleabane (Chugach Mts.)

BLACK-TIPPED GROUNDSEL

Senecio lugens

Family: Aster / Asteraceae

Habitat: Margins of bogs and fields, and in the tundra throughout most of Alaska.

Blooming Time: Late June to early August.

Description: A plant from 12 to 24" tall. Basal leaves quite rounded and shallowly toothed. Stem leaves becoming much longer. The bracts of the shaggy, daisy-type flowers are edged with black.

Comments: *Senecio pauciflorus* has more deeply toothed stem leaves and quite tight orange-colored flowers. *Senecio vulgaris* is an introduced species with very tight yellow flowers. There are many short groundsels (up to 8"), usually with single flowers. Most grow in damp tundra, are quite wooly when young, and bloom very early. *Senecio conterminus* (see drawing below), *Senecio cymbalarioides* and *Senecio pauperculus*, are shorter branched varieties (6 to 12" tall) found in dry areas of Interior and Eastern Alaska.

TRIANGULAR-LEAVED FLEABANE

Senecio triangularis

Family: Aster / Asteraceae

Habitat: Alpine meadows and stream banks in Southcentral and coastal Alaska including Kodiak Island.

Blooming Time: July and August.

Description: a large (2 to 2-1/2') plant with many triangular, toothed leaves that gradually become smaller up the stem. The ragged flowers are in flat-topped clusters.

MARSH FLEABANE , MASTODON FLOWER

Senecio congestus

Family: Daisy, Aster or Composite/ Asteraceae.

Habitat: Wetlands, marshes and lake margins throughout most of Alaska, except Southeastern and the Aleutian chain.

Blooming Time: July to early August.

Description: A tall (2-1/2 to 5') quite stout plant. Leaves are long and pointed, quite broad at the base, and have deeply cut teeth. Flower clusters are large, dense, wooly and light yellow.

Comments: There are 3 varieties in Alaska; all distinctive plants because of their very large flower heads:

Var. congestus (alpine) being short and very wooly.

Var. palustris (lowlands) being tall and not as hairy.

Var. tonsus being less hairy than either of the above.

Marsh Fleabane, Mastodon Flower (Glenn Hwy.)

BEACH FLEABANE

Senecio pseudo-arnica

Family: Daisy, Aster or Composite/ Asteraceae

Habitat: Sandy beaches in Southeastern, Southcentral and western coastal Alaska, and the Aleutian chain.

Blooming Time: July and August.

Description: A leafy robust plant 18 to 24" tall, with large flowers that are white and wooly in bud. Leaves are large oblanceolate, shallowly toothed, fleshy, green above and wooly white beneath. A distinctive plant because of growth pattern and habitat.

Beach Fleabane (Homer)

Alpine Arnica (Fairbanks)

Frigid Arnica (Healy)

Lessing's Arnica (Chugach Mts.)

ALPINE ARNICA

Arnica alpina, ssp. angustifolia

Family: Daisy, Aster, or Composite/ Asteraceae

Habitat: Dry alpine and sub-alpine slopes in Eastern Alaska and Interior and Northern Alaska north of Fairbanks.

Blooming Time: June & July.

Description: Upright perennial plant 7 to 12" tall with narrow pointed leaves that are sometimes slightly wavy along the edges. Flower stems have 1 to 3 sets of leaves. Flowers of *Arnicas* are large yellow daisy-type with broad ray flowers. Leaves are opposite and usually hairy.

Comments: Ssp. *attenuata* is taller and has a branched inflorescence. There are several *Arnicas* in Alaska. Frigid Arnica, *Arnica frigida*, is mostly an alpine plant. Most of its leaves are basal and broad, and flowers somewhat nodding. Another alpine plant, Lessing's Arnica, *Arnica Lessingii*, has mostly basal leaves, and pale yellow flowers that almost always nod. Meadow Arnica, *Arnica latifolia*, is a somewhat taller alpine meadow plant, and *Arnica amplexicaulis* and *Arnica chamissonis* are common taller meadow plants that have branched inflorescences. Meadow *Arnicas* bloom in July and August.

Meadow Arnica (Chugach Mts.)

WHITE & CREAM-FLOWERED PLANTS

Alpine Meadow, Hatcher Pass
Cow Parsnip, Sitka Burnet, Triangular leaf Fleabane, False Hellebore

COW PARSNIP
(Photo on previous page)

Heracleum lanatum

Family: Parsley / Apiaceae

Habitat: Moist fields, woodlands, and alpine meadows.

Blooming Time: July to mid-August.

Description: A tall (5 to 8 ') plant with large hollow stems and very large, somewhat palmate, leaves that are deeply divided into threes with deep extra incisions. Leaf stems connect to the main stalk with a clasping sheath. The leaves and stems have conspicuous hairs. The small flowers have 5 petals, are frequently covered with flying insects and are in double umbels. The seed heads are used for flower-arranging. The seeds are flat and are divided into 2 sections.

Comments: A distinctive plant because of its size. Leaves of young plants may sometimes be mistaken for Devil's Club which is a shrub with spines. The hairs on the leaves and stems are very irritating to some people's skin causing itching and rash. It may cause the skin to become overly sensitive to the sun (photosensitivity) causing severe sunburn with blisters which are very slow to heal. The peeled raw stems and the cooked roots are eaten by Native people.

Wild Celery (Kenai Peninsula)

WILD CELERY

Angelica lucida

Family: Celery / Apiaceae

Habitat: Riverbanks, meadows and coastal areas throughout Southeastern, coastal Southcentral, Central and Western Alaska.

Blooming Time: Late June and July.

Description: A rather stout plant, 18 to 36" tall. Very leafy with serrated leaflets and inflated, almost translucent petioles. Flowers are greenish-white and in an umbel.

Comments: Although edible, this plant is very strong tasting. *Angelica genuflexa* is a taller (4 to 7') species with purplish stems and petioles bent at a right angle to the main stem. Caution should be taken not to confuse it with the *Cicuta* genera which is poisonous. Hemlock Parsley, *Conioselinum chinense*, 2 to 4', which occurs in coastal areas, has very fine cut foliage and smaller flower heads. *Cnidium cnidifolium*, 1-1/2 to 2-1/2', also with very finely cut foliage, occurs in Interior Alaska.

Angelica genuflexa (Kenai Peninsula)

BEACH LOVAGE

Ligusticum scoticum

Family: Parsley / Apiaceae

Habitat: Seashores from Southeastern Alaska to the Seward Peninsula.

Blooming Time: Late June and July.

Description: A glabrous plant (15 to 24") with 3-parted, coarsely-toothed leaves. Lower stem is often purplish as are the leaf sheaths. The pinkish-white flowers are in double umbels

Comments: Leaves and stem can be eaten raw or cooked. Often seen in bloom and seed at the same time.

Beach Lovage (Potter's Marsh)

POISON WATER HEMLOCK

Cicuta Mackenzieana

Family: Parsley / Apiaceae

Habitat: Marshes and edges of lakes.

Blooming Time: July and August.

Description: Plant with 2-1/2 to 4' tall hollow stems. Leaves are compound, narrow and slightly notched. Petioles have a clasping base. Flowers are small, have 5 white petals and are arranged in double umbels.

Comments: **POISONOUS**. There are 3 members of the genus in Alaska. They have been mistaken for the *Angelica* genus which is edible, grows in similar areas and is commonly known as Wild Celery. To be sure which genus you have, it is best to cut the root lengthwise. Poison Hemlock has large wide transverse chambers separated by partitions. A yellow oily substance may also be seen when the root is cut. All parts of the plant are poisonous, but the roots particularly so. It may be easily seen growing around lakes and in the Eklutna Flats area just north of the village of Eklutna on the Glenn Highway north of Anchorage. It usually grows in the water, while *Angelica* usually grows in moist meadows and coastal areas. (If you do cut a root open to look at it, be very sure to wash your knife thoroughly before using it for cutting any food!!!)

Poison Water Hemlock (Kenai Peninsula)

Poison Water Hemlock root   Marilyn Barker
(Kenai Peninsula)

Wild Rhubarb (Alaska Hwy., Fairbanks)

WILD RHUBARB

Polygonum alaskanum

Family: Buckwheat / Polygonaceae

Habitat: Roadsides and open woods in Interior and Western Alaska.

Blooming Time: July and early August.

Description: A tall (2 to 5') perennial with a thick root and a somewhat woody, branched stem. The oblanceolate leaves are smooth, entire, medium green above and lighter beneath. The tiny flowers are yellowish-white and in a dense branched panicle.

Comments: Young stems and leaves may be eaten, raw or cooked.

Goatsbeard (Turnagain Arm)

GOATSBEARD

Aruncus sylvester

Family: Rose / Rosaceae

Habitat: Moist, open woods, meadows and along streams; mostly in coastal areas.

Blooming Time: July

Description: A tall perennial plant, 24 to 48" tall, with bi-pinnate toothed leaves. Each leaflet looks like an individual leaf; the combined, somewhat like rose leaves. The cream-colored flowers are tiny and on long branched spikes above the leaves. Very distinctive in bloom. Male and female flowers are on separate plants. The male (pollen producing) flowers are larger and more showy.

Comments: May be confused with Baneberry in early Spring, but Goatsbeard leaves and stem have a reddish cast. Baneberry foliage is dark, somewhat blackish. Very common along the Seward Highway from Bird Creek to Girdwood.

SITKA VALERIAN

Valeriana sitchensis

Family: Valerian / Valerianaceae

Habitat: Moist meadows in Southcentral, Eastern and Southeastern Alaska.

Blooming Time: July and August.

Description: A tall plant, 18 to 24", often having a few hairs. Most leaves are on its flower stem, are opposite, and have 5 segments; higher up the stem they have 3 segments and are reduced in size. The edges of the leaves are wavy. The small flaring, tubular flowers are in rounded, loose heads and are sometimes light pinkish in bud. The bracts in the flower head are slightly hairy.

Sitka Valerian (Hatcher Pass)

Lower leaves

CAPITATE VALERIAN

Valeriana capitata

Family: Valerian / Valerianaceae

Habitat: Moist woods, heaths and tundra throughout most of Alaska, except southern Southeastern.

Blooming Time: June and July.

Description: A mostly glabrous plant (5" to 12" tall) with dark green leaves. Basal leaves are ovate. The stem leaves are wavy, the lower ones divided into 3 leaflets (the middle one being long and pointed). Upper stem leaves are entire and nearly linear. Bracts in flower heads are glabrous. The tight, round flower head is maroon in bud, turning pink to pinkish-white, then white in full bloom.

Capitate Valerian (Chugach Mts.)

Basal leaves

Alp Lily   Marilyn Barker
(Chugach Mts.)

ALP LILY

Lloydia serotina

Family: Lily / Liliaceae

Habitat: Dry alpine areas throughout most of Alaska.

Blooming Time: June

Description: A very small (4 to 6") alpine plant with narrow, grass-like leaves. The flowers have 3 petals and 3 sepals which look nearly alike (giving the appearance of 6 pointed petals). They are white (brownish on the underside). The delicate plants have one or two, 1/2" to 3/4" funnel-shaped flowers per stem.

Comments: Unmistakable--the only small plant of its kind in Alaska.

Baneberry (Turnagain Arm)

BANEBERRY, SNAKEBERRY

Actaea rubra

Family: Crowfoot / Ranunculaceae

Habitat: Woodlands south of the Brooks Range.

Blooming Time: Late May to early June.

Description: Erect, perennial plant (18 to 30") with fairly large compound, 3 to 5-parted, toothed leaves. All leaves have long stems that grow from the main flower stalk. The delicate white flowers are small and in rounded clusters. The red or white, long stemmed clusters of berries are high above the leaves and ripen from mid-July through August. The berries are opaque, have an indentation or crease down one side (like a peach) and a black dot at the end.

Comments: CAUTION-- HIGHLY POISONOUS. The ingestion of as few as 6 berries has been known to cause death in a small child. Found frequently along the mountain sides from Palmer to Girdwood. Easily seen from pulloffs along the Seward Highway, espe-

Baneberry (Turnagain Arm)

cially at McHugh Creek Wayside (about 7 miles south of Anchorage).

MOUNTAIN ASH

Sorbus sitchensis

Family: Rose / Rosaceae

Habitat: Woods, low alpine meadows and slopes in Southeastern, coastal Southcentral Alaska and Cook Inlet area.

Blooming Time: June

Description: A shrubby tree up to 9 feet tall with reddish bark. Young twigs have rusty colored hairs. The leaves are arranged alternately on the stems and are pinnately divided into 7 to 11 notched leaflets. The small flowers are 5-petaled and in rounded, rather flat clusters at the ends of branches. Large, round, reddish-orange berries with a bluish bloom are obvious in the Fall and are a favorite food of the Bohemian Waxwings.

Comments: The flat flower heads and berry clusters distinguish it easily from the confusing species, Red-berried Elder, *Sambucus racemosa*. The berries of Mt. Ash can be used as food, but are bitter until frozen and thawed a few times. This happens naturally on the tree. They may be stewed and sweetened for a tasty winter fruit. Four species of Mountain Ash are native to Alaska. Another common species seen is Green Mountain Ash, *Sorbus scopulina*, having 11-13 leaflets, young twigs with whitish hairs, and orange to red, glossy berries. European Mountain Ash, *Sorbus aucuparia*, which is frequently seen in city plantings is a small tree native to Europe, that has escaped from cultivation in Southeastern Alaska.

Mountain Ash (Turnagain Arm)

Red-berried Elder (Turnagain Arm)

RED-BERRIED ELDER

Sambucus racemosa

Family: Honeysuckle / Caprifoliaceae

Habitat: Woods and subalpine meadows in Southeastern, coastal Southcentral Alaska, and the Aleutian Chain.

Blooming Time: June

Description: A tall shrub (5 to 9') with opposite branches and soft pithy stems becoming brown and warty-looking. Young branches are purplish and have 5 to 7 toothed, oval, pointed leaflets. Flowers are tiny, 5-petaled, creamy-white in a pyramidal raceme. Ill scented shrub and flowers. Fruit is small, bright orange to red, ripening in August.

Comments: CAUTION—All parts of Elderberry except the pulp of the berries and flowers are poisonous. However, the poison is broken down by boiling.

Red-berried Elder, berry (Turnagain Arm)

Alaska Spiraea (Anchorage)

ALASKA SPIRAEA, BEAUVERD'S SPIRAEA

Spiraea Beauverdiana

Family: Rose / Rosaceae

Habitat: Woodland and alpine slopes throughout most of Alaska, except the North Slope and coastal Southeastern Alaska.

Blooming Time: June to July.

Description: A low to medium sized shrub (10 to 30", depending on elevation) with delicate reddish-brown branches. The oblong leaves have fine teeth especially near the tip. They are dark green and nearly hairless on top and pale beneath. The small, 5-petalled white flowers are in small flat-topped clusters. Easily recognized in Winter by its flat-topped brown seen heads.

Comments: Leaves may be brewed into a tea.

ALPINE SPIRAEA

Luetkea pectinata

Family: Rose / Rosaceae

Habitat: Sub-alpine heaths and alpine slopes in Southeastern and Southcentral Alaska, including Kodiak Island and the Eastern Aleutians.

Blooming Time: Late June to mid-August.

Description: A sub-shrub (4 to 7") with fine ferny type rosettes near the base and smaller dissected leaves continuing up the flowering stem. Flowers are small, 5-petalled, creamy-white and clustered at the end of the stalks. It forms large moss-like mats usually in moist areas or on the North side of slopes. The mats frequently cover large boulders.

Comments: A distinctive plant, but could be mistaken for a moss at a casual glance.

Alpine Spiraea (Hatcher Pass)

SITKA BURNET

Sanguisorba stipulata
Family: Rose / Rosaceae
Habitat: Bogs and meadows throughout the southern half of Alaska including the Alaska Range.
Blooming Time: July and August.
Description: A perennial plant having a flowering stem 1 to 2' tall with a few small leaves. The long stemmed basal leaves consist of many glabrous, toothed ovate leaflets. It has a spike of many tiny flowers with 5 greenish-white sepals, no petals and many long stamens.

Comments: Two maroon colored Burnets are found in Alaska. They generally grow at low elevations. *Sanguisorba officianalis* has very short stamens and *Sanguisorba Menziesii* has long maroon stamens--an impressive plant. The leaves of all of these plants may be eaten when young, but become tough with maturity.

Sitka Burnet (Anchorage)

ALPINE MEADOW BISTORT

Polygonum viviparum
Family: Buckwheat / Polygonaceae
Habitat: Dry meadows, heaths and tundra throughout Alaska.
Blooming Time: June and July.
Description: A variable plant (5 to 8") with long, narrow entire leaves arising from a thick, hard rhizome. The top surface of the leaves are dark green and glabrous, the undersides are grayish. The tiny 5-petalled flowers are white to pinkish and are rapidly replaced by bulblets sprouting leaves and roots before they fall from the adult plant.
Comments: The boiled roots are

Alpine Meadow Bistort (Chugach Mts.)

a good starch food source and the leaves may be eaten raw or cooked.

Northern Bedstraw (Anchorage)

Sweet-scented Bedstraw (Turnagain Arm)

Grass of Parnassus (Anchorage)

NORTHERN BEDSTRAW

Galium boreale

Family: Madder / Rubiaceae

Habitat: Woodlands and meadows throughout most of Alaska, except Southeastern and the North Slope.

Blooming Time: July to early August.

Description: An erect, branched perennial (12 to 20" tall) having square stems with intervals of 4 leaves in whorls around stem. The leaves are long and pointed with 3 linear veins that appear parallel. Flowers are numerous, very small and have 4 white petals.

Comments: The plant was used in early times as mattress stuffing because it is sweet scented and its square stems did not crush easily. There are several bedstraws in Alaska. The rest are weak, trailing woodland plants with inconspicuous flowers and more rounded leaves. Sweet-scented Bedstraw, *Galium triflorum,* is a common weak stemmed, woodland variety usually having 3 flowers per stem section and 6 leaves in each whorl.

GRASS OF PARNASSUS, BOG STAR

Parnassia palustris

Family: Saxifrage / Saxifragaceae

Habitat: Wet meadows, roadside ditches and lake margins throughout most of Alaska, except the Aleutian Chain.

Blooming Time: July and August.

Description: A perennial plant growing in a small clump with small, nearly heart-shaped, yellowish-green leaves at the base. Flower stems are long (5 to 15") with one smaller modified leaf and one (3/4 to 1") 5-petaled flower per stem. The petals are pointed and conspicuously veined. The center and seed capsule are prominently pointed.

Comments: This late blooming flower is not easily confused with any other. Small Grass of Parnassus, *Parnassia kotzebuei*, is a wet alpine plant, and is much smaller with small petaled flowers. Fringed Grass of Parnassus, *Parnassia fimbriata,* is a late-blooming alpine variety (6 to 12" tall) with fine white hair-like fringe on the petals.

DWARF DOGWOOD, BUNCHBERRY, CANADIAN DWARF CORNEL

Cornus canadensis

Family: Dogwood / Cornaceae

Habitat: Woods, tundra, and low alpine areas.

Blooming Time: Woodlands-June, Alpine-July.

Description: A low herbaceous shrub, 4 to 8" tall, with one small pair of leaves near the base and a whorl of leaves at the top having prominent arched veins. The flowers are in a cluster set off by 4 white bracts, each flower having 4 greenish sepals. A bunch of orange or reddish berries are seen in August and September.

Dwarf Dogwood (Anchorage)

Edibility: Questionable, but not dangerous. The Pilgrims made a pudding out of the berries, but some people complained of stomach upsets after eating large quantities.

Comments: A similar species, Swedish Dwarf Cornel, *Cornus suecica*, has reddish-purple flowers and all leaves in pairs. Hybridization between the two species is very common. Red Twig Dogwood, *Cornus stolonifera*, is a tall (4 to 9') shrub found in woods and having bunches of very small flowers followed by white berries that are poisonous. Winter twigs are very red. Although the actual flowers are not white, these plants were included in this section because the white bracts look like petals.

Swedish Dwarf Cornel (Chugach Mts.)

Red Twig Dogwood (Matanuska Valley)

Bunch berries (Anchorage)

Kamchatka Rockcress (Turnagain Arm)

Holboell's Rockcress (Turnagain Arm)

Starflower (Anchorage)

KAMCHATKA ROCKCRESS

Arabis lyrata

Family: Mustard / Brassicaceae

Habitat: Dry, open woodlands at low to mid elevations throughout most of Alaska.

Blooming Time: Late May thru June.

Description: A low plant (6 to 9" tall) with a long taproot (typical of mustard family). Lower basal leaves are toothed (like Dandelion). Upper and stem leaves are entire in margin. The small white flowers have 4 petals and 6 stamens.

Comments: Edible leaves. Several species of *Arabis* are found in Alaska, most having a rosette of hairy, lanceolate leaves, small white to pinkish flowers on stems far above the rosette, and seeds in a silique or silicle. A taller similar introduced species, Shepherd's Purse, *Capsella Bursa-pastoris*, has heart-shaped seed pods and is common in lawns. Holboell's Rockcress, *Arabis Holboelli*, is very common on dry slopes. It has lavender to white, bell-shaped flowers on a 6 to 24" tall stem arising from a rosette of hairy leaves.

Kamchatka
Rockcress

Holboell's
Rockcress

STARFLOWER

Trientalis europea ssp arctica

Family: Primrose / Primulaceae

Habitat: Woodlands and low alpine slopes throughout most of Alaska south of the Brooks Range.

Blooming Time: June to early July.

Description: A low perennial with reddish runners. The oval pointed (often reddish) leaves are in a whorl around the stem. The flowers usually have 7 pointed white petals and the seed is a small silver ball.

Comments: An easily recognized plant. Another sub-species, *europaea*, has narrower, more pointed leaves.

MOUSE EAR CHICKWEED

Cerastrium arvense

Family: Pink / Caryophyllaceae

Habitat: Dry, rocky hillsides, coastal areas and alpine areas in Southcentral and Southeastern Alaska, and the Aleutian Chain.

Blooming Time: June and July.

Description: A low, mat-forming (5 to 8") plant with opposite, narrow, hairy, silvery leaves. Flowers are 3/4" across and have 5 rounded and notched white petals that are 2 to 3 times longer than the sepals. This plant has sterile side shoots (non-flowering branches in axile of uppermost leaves).

Comments: Mouse Ear Chickweed may be seen easily on the rocky areas along the Seward Highway south from Anchorage. A similar species, *Cerastrium Beeringianum var. grandiflorum*, does not have sterile side shoots and its petals are only twice as long as sepals. *Cerastrium maximum* is a very tall plant (18 to 30") with large (1 to 1/2") flowers and is found in Central Alaska.

Mouse Ear Chickweed (Seward Hwy.)

Grove Sandwort (Seward Hwy.)

GROVE SANDWORT

Moehringia lateriflora

Family: Pink / Caryophyllaceae

Habitat: Woodlands and alpine slopes. Very common throughout most of Alaska, except the North Slope.

Blooming Time: Late May and June.

Description: A small, rather delicate, upright plant (4 to 7" tall) with small, opposite, oval leaves. The small flowers have 5 white petals.

Comments: This plant is easily mistaken for a Chickweed (*Stellaria*) which has 5 petals, each split, appearing to be 10. There are several *Stellarias* in Alaska and they grow in similar locations.

Stellaria (Seward Hwy.)

Pussy Toes (Seward Hwy.)

Cat's Paw (Hatcher Pass)

Prickly Saxifrage (Seward Hwy.)

PUSSY TOES

Antennaria sp.

Family: Aster or Daisy / Asteraceae

Habitat: Dry, open woodlands; and, More commonly in alpine areas.

Blooming Time: June.

Description: A low, mat-forming plant with silvery appearance. Leaves are small, usually lance to oval shape in rosettes spreading by underground runners. Flowers are on a 3 to 6" silky, hairy stem and consist of several button-like flower heads (hence its common name).

Comments: Easily recognized by its low mat of silvery rosettes. There are many species in Alaska separated by minor characteristics. Some are pink. Cat's Paw, *Antennaria monocephala,* is a white alpine species having greener, less hairy leaves and white flower heads. Pussy Toes are common in rocky areas along the Seward Highway just south of Anchorage.

PRICKLY SAXIFRAGE

Saxifraga tricuspidata

Family: Saxifrage / Saxifragaceae

Habitat: Dry, rocky, open sub-alpine and alpine slopes.

Blooming Time: Late May to mid-June.

Description: A low, loosely-matted, evergreen plant with rosettes of small, wedge-shaped, thick, somewhat fleshy leaves having 3 sharply pointed prongs on the ends. During dry seasons, they become very sharp and prickly. During the Winter and in early Spring, the leaves are very red. The lower part of the stems contain many dried up old leaves. The flower stem (4 to 6") is quite stout, light in color and has a few small modified leaves . The stems are topped with a cluster of small flowers with protruding ovaries. Each flower has 5 lavender spotted, sharply-pointed, cream-colored petals.

Comments: Sometimes confused with Yellow Spotted Saxifrage, see page 39 (Yellow Section).

BROOK SAXIFRAGE

Saxifraga punctata

Family: Saxifrage / Saxifragaceae

Habitat: Wet meadows, lake margins and woodlands, especially near streams, throughout most of Alaska.

Blooming Time: June and July.

Description: Alaska has several varieties ranging from 5 to 12" in height, having fleshy, kidney-shaped, triangular, toothed basal leaves, and a spike of small 5-petalled, 10-stamen flowers and reddish seed capsules.

Comments: Alaska has many similar *Saxifrages* that grow in wet areas. All have edible leaves. Some of these are: Bulblet Saxifrage, *Saxifraga cernua*, which has smaller but similar leaves that continue up the stem, white flowers on top, and red bulblets (new plants) along the stem. Alpine Brook Saxifrage, *Saxifraga rivularis*, has tiny leaves and flowers. Red-stemmed Saxifrage, *Saxifraga Lyallii*, has leaves that are toothed on the end, but wedge-shaped at the base and a very red stem. Coast Saxifrage, *Saxifraga ferruginea*, has wedge-shaped leaves and grows in coastal areas of Southcentral Alaska. All saxifrages have an obvious ovary in the center of the flower.

Brook Saxifrage (Hatcher Pass)

Coast Saxifrage (Thompson Pass)

Red-stemmed Saxifrage (Hatcher Pass)

Bulblet Saxifrage (EagleSummit)

Labrador Tea (Anchorage)

Leather Leaf (Anchorage)

Large-flowered Wintergreen (Glenn Hwy.)

LABRADOR TEA

Ledum palustris ssp groenlandicum

Family: Heath / Ericaceae

Habitat: Heaths, bogs, woods and alpine slopes in Southeastern, Central and Southcentral Alaska.

Blooming Time: June

Description: Low to medium height evergreen shrub (10 to 30") with a rusty pubescence on young twigs and under side of leaves. Leaves are green, long, oblong with edges rolled under. Leaves are brownish and leathery in the winter. The small flowers are 5-petaled usually having 10 stamens.

Comments: Distinctive plant because of rusty hairs on stems and aromatic odor. *Ledum palustre ssp. decumbens* (Narrow-leaf Labrador Tea) is somewhat smaller, has very narrow leaves, sometimes pinkish flowers, and is found in bogs and alpine heaths throughout most of the State. The ledum genus contains "ledol", a poison causing cramps and acting as a diuretic. A tasty tea is made of the leaves, but should be taken sparingly at first, until the system adjusts to its effects. Leatherleaf, *Chamaedaphne calyculata,* is a shrub with a similar appearance but with white urn-shaped flowers. It blooms in May. The leaves are elongated, oval and evergreen. They are brown and leathery in the Winter and Spring, greenish in the Summer.

LARGE-FLOWERED WINTERGREEN

Pyrola grandiflora

Family: Wintergreen / Pyrolaceae

Habitat: Woodlands and dry places on the tundra, and in the mountains throughout most of Alaska, except the Aleutian Chain, Southeastern Alaska, and coastal areas of Southcentral and Southwestern Alaska.

Blooming Time: June and early July.

Description: An evergreen plant having thick, glossy, large, round, slightly wavy basal leaves. The 5-petalled white flowers are 1/2 to 3/4", have pinkish veins, and are clustered at the top of 5 to 10" tall thick stems. Typical of pyrolas, they have a pronounced style that curves at maturity. The seed capsule is round and has 5 sections with a protruding style.

SINGLE DELIGHT, SHY MAIDEN

Moneses uniflora

Family: Wintergreen / Pyrolaceae

Habitat: Woods throughout most of Alaska except the North Slope, the Aleutian Chain and western coastal areas.

Blooming Time: June and July.

Description: A small plant with a rosette of small, light green, roundish leaves (about 1/2") with shallow teeth. The flower is on a leafless stem 2-1/2 to 4" high and has 5 pointed, waxy petals. It has a protruding ovary and faces downward. The capsule is round with protruding stigma.

Comments: A distinctive plant frequently found with other pyrolas--very fragrant. There are 2 varieties in Alaska. Variety *reticulata* is seen in coastal areas and has slightly larger leaves with deeper serrations.

Single Delight (Anchorage)

DEATH CAMAS, CAMAS WAND LILY

Zygadenus elegans

Family: Lily / Liliaceae

Habitat: Open woods and meadows throughout most of Alaska, except extreme Southeastern and Southwestern areas.

Blooming Time: Late June to early August.

Description: A bulbous perennial plant, 12 to 18" tall, with narrow, strap-like, slightly bluish-green leaves that appear folded down the center line. The flowers are well spaced on a raceme on a long stem and are greenish-yellow to cream-colored. Each flower has 6 tepals (3 petals & 3 sepals that look alike). There is a bract or reduced leaf at the base of each petiole.

Comments: **EXTREME CAUTION** **Highly toxic poison** which causes vomiting, lowered temperatures and breathing difficulties.

Death Camas (Glenn Hwy.)

Buckbean (Glenn Hwy., Palmer area)

BUCKBEAN / BOG BEAN
Menyanthes trifoliata

Family: Bogbean / Menyanthaceae

Habitat: Lakes, ponds, marshes and bogs throughout most of Alaska, except the North Slope.

Blooming Time: Late May to mid June.

Description: A plant, usually growing in water, with flower spikes above its leaves and the water. Leaves are glabrous, divided into 3 ovate leaflets. Flowers have 5 white to pinkish petals with white hairs along the margins giving it a fringed look. Very aromatic.

Comments: A distinctive plant as it blooms very early, and in standing water. Easily seen in marshy area just south of the Parks Highway cutoff on the Glenn Highway.

WILD CALLA
Calla palustris

Family: Arum / Araceae

Habitat: Margins of lakes and ponds mostly in Interior Alaska and a few scattered areas of the Matanuska Valley and the Kenai Peninsula.

Blooming Time: July and August.

Description: A thick stemmed plant with elongated, thick, shiny, heart-shaped leaves arising from a thick creeping rhizome. The tiny greenish flowers surround a short, thick stem arising from a white spathe (modified leaf). They are followed by light red berries.

Comments: The whole plant is poisonous, especially the berries. They contain saponin-like substances and poisonous acids. Although the poisons are neutralized by boiling or drying, it is **not** recommended that they be eaten. An unmistakable plant; although the actual flowers are not white, it was included in this section because the white spathe looks like a petal.

Wild Calla (Kenai)

ALASKA COTTON

Eriophorum Scheuchzeri

Family: Sedge / Cyperaceae

Habitat: Wet, peaty soil, margins of lakes. Shallow water and roadside ditches throughout Alaska.

Blooming Time: June and July.

Description: A stiff, erect plant (12 to 15" tall) with narrow, linear grass-like leaves. The flower stalk has one seed head with long white bristles.

Comments: There are 14 species of Cotton Grass in Alaska. *Eriophorum russeolum* is a similar species with slightly rust-colored bristles. Tall Cotton Grass, *Eriophorum angustifolium,* is a taller species with 3 to 5 drooping heads. It is found throughout the State. The lower stems of Tall Cotton Grass are edible and tasty, as are the roots. The Eskimos raid mouse caches for these tasty tidbits, called "Mouse Nuts".

Alaska Cotton (Kenai Peninsula)

Tall Cotton Grass (Anchorage)

ARCTIC DAISY

Chrysanthemum arcticum ssp. arcticum

Family: Aster / Asteraceae

Habitat: Rocky coastal areas and marshes in Southeastern, Southcentral, and Western Alaska, and the Aleutian Chain.

Blooming Time: July.

Description: The notched and blunt-toothed leaves are dark green, glabrous, and are reduced in size and divisions as they proceed up the 8 to 18" tall stem. Ray flowers are broad.

Comments: Subspecies *polare* is a much shorter arctic variety. *Chrysanthemum integrifolium,* a small alpine plant with narrow leaves, that may be white, pink or lavender. Wild Arctic Camomile, *Tripleurospermum phaeocephalum,* which grows in coastal areas of Northwestern Alaska and the North Slope, has fine, feathery foliage like Pineapple Weed. (See page 40). All other white daisies seen along the highways or in disturbed areas are introduced plants.

Arctic Daisy (Kenai Peninsula)

Arctic Sandwort and Moss Campion (Arctic Valley)

Mountain Avens (Hatcher Pass)

Mountain Avens, seed head (Hatcher Pass)

ARCTIC SANDWORT

Minuartia arctica

Family: Pink / Caryophyllaceae

Habitat: Dry, gravelly and rocky alpine areas throughout Central, Southcentral and coastal Alaska.

Blooming Time: June to early July.

Description: A low mat-forming plant with very narrow, small leaves. Flowers are singular (1/2 to 3/4") on short stems and have 5 petals, occasionally slightly rosy.

Comments: There are several *Minuartias* in Alaska, but most are more delicate, less mat-forming plants and have smaller flowers.

MOUNTAIN AVENS, EIGHT-PETALED AVENS

Dryas octopetala

Family: Rose / Rosaceae

Habitat: Tundra and high alpine slopes.

Blooming Time: June.

Description: A mat-forming shrub with coarse, oblong leaves with fairly even, wavy indentations, the edges slightly rolled under. The top side bluish-green and the underside silvery from hairs. The flowers usually have 8 long petals, the stamens are bright yellow. When the flowers go to seed, they have a characteristic twist and then progress into a seed head much like a dandelion.

Comments: *Dryas integrifolia* is very similar, but has entire leaves. Hybrids between the 2 species are common. *Dryas Drummondii* is a similar appearing plant of lower elevations with yellow, nodding flowers. It is common near the village of Eklutna and other sunny, gravelly areas and stream beds. See page 28 in Yellow Section.

NARCISSUS-FLOWERED ANEMONE

Anemone narcissiflora

Family: Buttercup / Ranunculaceae

Habitat: Alpine meadows and slopes, and slightly subalpine open woodlands throughout most of Alaska.

Blooming Time: June through mid-August.

Description: A somewhat hairy, clumping perennial plant (8 to 14" tall) having deeply dissected, 3 to 5-lobed, hairy leaves on long stems arising from the base of plants. The showy (1 to 2") flowers are on stems above the leaves and are variable. They have 4 to 10 white, somewhat acute sepals usually with a slight bluish cast on the underside. The modified leaf on the stem below the flowers completely surrounds the stem; a characteristic of Anemones and Pasque flower.

Comments: Subspecies *villosima* may be found growing close to sea level in coastal areas. Windflower, *Anemone parviflora,* has more rounded glabrous leaves, blooms very early and almost always has 5 large rounded (over 1"), white sepals that are quite bluish on the underside. It blooms as soon as the snow leaves and is found in moist woodlands, alpine meadows and snow flushes. Cut-leaf Anemone, *Anemone multifida*, has more finely and deeply cut, hairy leaves and smaller flowers (3/4 to 1") that are creamy inside and rosy or lavender underneath. It grows in dry, open woodlands and hillsides.

Narcissus-flowered Anemone (Denali Hwy.)

Windflower (Chugach Mts.)

Cut-leaf Anemone (Turnagain Arm)

Windflower, underside of sepals

Moss Heather (Hatcher Pass)

Bell Heather (North Slope)   James Wallace, Jr.

ALPINE HEUCHERA

Heuchera glabra

Family: Saxifrage / Saxifragaceae

Habitat: Moist, rocky areas in Southeastern, Southcentral Alaska and the Aleutian Chain.

Blooming Time: June and July.

Description: A clumping, perennial plant with 3 to 5-lobed, toothed, long stemmed, coarse, basal leaves that are slightly hairy beneath and around the edges. Old dead stems are often present at the base. The tiny, white, 5-petaled flowers are grouped in 3s along the branched 10 to 16" stem.

MOSS HEATHER

Cassiope stelleriana

Family: Heath / Ericaceae

Habitat: Mountain slopes (frequently the north side) and moist woodlands near the coast of Southeastern and Southcentral Alaska and the Aleutian Chain.

Blooming Time: June and July.

Description: A matted dwarf evergreen shrub (6 to 8" tall) looking much like Crowberry or moss. Leaves are very narrow and yellowish-green. The campanulate flowers which are composed of 5 joined, slightly flared, white petals are singular with short stems, occasionally pinkish. Sepals are reddish.

Comments: Heather has an overpowering aroma; pleasant at a distance. There are several Heathers in Alaska. The Mountain Heather, *Phyllodoce* species, has urn-shaped flowers and longer leaves. Bell Heather, *Cassiope tetragona*, has hanging white flowers and leaves in 4 stacking rows, causing the branches to look like a Phillips screwdriver. A distinctive plant.

Alpine Heuchera (Turnagain Arm)

CLOUDBERRY, BAKED APPLEBERRY, SALMONBERRY

Rubus chamemorous

Family: Rose / Rosaceae

Habitat: Bogs and tundra.

Blooming Time: Late May and June.

Description: A low, herbaceous plant having coarse veined, long stemmed, leaves with 5 lobes and 1" flowers with 5 (sometimes 4) rounded white petals (much like an apple blossom). The tasty, orange, raspberry-like berries, which ripen in mid-July to early August, are not produced in abundance. They look much like a cluster of salmon eggs and taste a bit like a baked apple.

Cloudberry (Anchorage)

Comments: This is called Salmonberry by some Alaska natives. However, true Salmonberry, *Rubus spectabilis* (see page 16), grows much like raspberry canes (3 to 7' tall), has pink 5-petaled flowers and a berry similar to Cloudberry, but larger and longer. Confusing species are Nagoonberry, *Rubus arcticus*, (see page 16) and Trailing Raspberry, *Rubus pedatus*, which has 5 separate leaflets and white flowers with 5 narrow petals. It is found in moist, mossy woodlands and alpine areas. Berries ripen from August to September.

Cloudberry (Chugach Mts.)

Trailing Raspberry (Eklutna)   Marilyn Barker

Trailing Raspberry (Chugach Mts.)

Alpine Bearberry (Bison Gulch)

Alpine Bearberry (Chugach Mts.)

ALPINE BEARBERRY

Arctostaphylos alpina

Family: Heath / Ericaceae

Habitat: Rocky alpine areas and the tundra throughout most of Alaska, except Southeastern and the Yukon River drainage.

Blooming Time: Mid May to early June.

Description: A very low (up to 4") deciduous, branched shrub forming large mats with spatulate-shaped leaves that are course, leathery, and have hairs along the margins. Flowers are white, urn-shaped and bloom as the leaves are opening; occasionally before, amongst old dried leaves. The black, juicy, dull-looking berries are edible, but not widely used. The leaves turn bright red in the Fall, making a colorful scene in many tundra and alpine areas.

Comments: *Arctostaphylos rubra*, Red Bearberry, has less coarse leaves and no hairs on the margins and grows in bogs and moist meadows below treeline. It has red berries and yellow leaves in the Fall.

Fall foliage (Chugach Mts.)

Red Bearberry (Kenai Peninsula)

LOW-BUSH CRANBERRY, LINGONBERRY, MOUNTAIN CRANBERRY

Vaccinium vitis idaea

Family: Heath / Ericaceae

Habitat: Acidic soil, hummocks in bogs, woods and alpine slopes to about 3500 foot elevation, throughout the State.

Blooming Time: June and July (alpine).

Description: A low evergreen shrub arising from creeping horizontal roots with 3 to 8" upright branches with many shiny, oval, hard, evergreen leaves with rolled-over edges. The pink and white (color is very variable) small bell-shaped flowers are clustered at the end of the branches and produce tasty, firm, round, maroon berries that are used for jelly and baked goods. Usually ripe in early September, the flavor is best after a frost.

Comments: A true Bog Cranberry, *Oxycoccus microcarpus*, is a trailing, evergreen common in boggy areas and is recognized by its tiny leaves and light pink, reflexed flowers that look like miniature light-colored Shooting Stars. See drawing below.

KINNIKINNICK

Arctostaphylos uva-ursi

Family: Heath / Ericaceae

Habitat: Dry woods and dry, open, exposed sites throughout most of Alaska, except Southeastern and Northwest Alaska.

Blooming Time: Mid-may to mid-June.

Description: A sprawling evergreen shrub, with a main tap root, forming large mats with rounded spatulate leaves that are smooth and leathery above, and rough and lighter colored beneath. Flowers are small, pinkish-white and urn-shaped. Berries are reddish-orange, dry, mealy, and not used for food. Their taste and texture is often compared to a mouthful of lint.

Comments: Sometimes confused with Lowbush Cranberry, *Vaccinium vitis-idaea*, which sends up 3 to 8" upright branches from horizontal roots.

Low Bush Cranberry (Anchorage)

Low Bush Cranberry (Anchorage)

Kinnikinnick (Turnagain Arm)

Frigid Coltsfoot (Denali Hwy.)

Arrowleaf Coltsfoot (Fairbanks)

Alpine Milk Vetch (Glenallen)

FRIGID COLTSFOOT

Petasites frigidus

Family: Aster / Asteraceae

Habitat: Wet meadows and tundra, throughout most of Alaska, except Southeastern.

Blooming Time: Late May to mid-June.

Description: This plant frequently blooms before the leaves develop and has a very stout, hairy, blooming stalk with a cluster of white to pinkish flowers on top. This species could easily be placed in the Pink Section of this book. The dark green leaves are grayish beneath and shaped much like a horse's hoof, having wavy indentations. They are large (4 to 6" across) and soon develop long petioles. When mature, the flower stalk can be 12 to 16" tall and is probably more obvious when in seed. it looks much like a cluster of loose Cotton Grass or dense white Dandelion-like seed heads.

Comments: The leaves have been used in the past by Indians as a seasoning. The leaves were burned and the resulting ash used as a salt substitute. Leaves may be chopped and cooked, but are quite tough. Northern Coltsfoot, *Petasites hyperboreus*, is similar with deeper lobed leaves. Arrowleaf Coltsfoot, *Petasites sagitus,* which is common in Interior and Eastern Alaska, has triangular shaped leaves.

ALPINE MILK VETCH

Astragalus alpinus

Family: Pea / Fabaceae

Habitat: Roadsides, fields, dry open woodlands, and alpine slopes throughout most of Alaska.

Blooming Time: June and July.

Description: A low, creeping, matted plant with weak stems. The pinnately divided leaves have many small, somewhat acute tipped, oval leaflets. The small pea shaped flowers are white near the base and blue to lavender at the tip, oftentimes almost all blue. They are clustered in a short raceme at the end of the 4 to 8" stems.

Comments: This plant could easily be placed in the Blue to Violet Section of this book.

SERVICEBERRY, JUNEBERRY

Amelanchier florida
Family: Rose / Rosaceae
Habitat: Rocky, coastal, sub-alpine slopes.
Blooming Time: Late May to mid June.
Description: A shrub up to 12 feet tall, shorter in exposed, dry sites. Leaves are 1-1/2 to 2-1/2", with teeth around the obovate, rounded tip and having a distinct crease along the center. Flowers have 5 narrow petals in terminal racemes. The sweet edible berries, which look a bit like a small apple, are dark purplish-blue when ripe. The seeds are large and triangular which limits their use. The berries may be dried like raisins, and made into jellies or a pie. They ripen in early September and remain on the shrub until dry.

Comments: May easily be seen on rocky cliffs on Seward Highway south of Anchorage, just south of McHugh Creek. *Amelanchier alnifolia* has more rounded leaves and is found in similar areas. Occasionally confused with Blueberries or Huckleberries, which have untoothed leaves and are lacking the pronounced "blossom end" to the berry.

Serviceberry (Turnagain Arm)

Serviceberry (Turnagain Arm)

NORTHERN YARROW

Achillea borealis
Family: Aster / Asteraceae
Habitat: Roadsides, fields, dry open woods and alpine meadows and low alpine slopes throughout most of Alaska.
Blooming Time: July through August.
Description: A weedy perennial plant with fine, ferny 2 to 3 times pinnately dissected leaves which are variable in length and width. Somewhat reduced in size as they progress up the stem. They have an easily recognized flat-topped cluster of small, white (sometimes pinkish) flowers. The flat-topped brown seed heads are used for flower-arranging. The involucre of bracts are rounded and have a dark margin.

Comments: Very common along highways. The aromatic leaves are used as a pot herb and to make a soothing, pleasing tea. *Achillea sibirica* has long, narrow leaves with deep serrations and is found more in Interior Alaska.

Northern Yarrow (Anchorage)

High-bush Cranberry (Anchorage)

High-bush Cranberry (Anchorage)

Wild Strawberry (Fairbanks)

HIGH-BUSH CRANBERRY

Viburnum edule

Family: Honeysuckle / Caprifoliaceae

Habitat: Woods and alpine areas up to at least 2500 feet, throughout most of Alaska, except the North Slope, western Coastal Alaska and the Aleutian Chain.

Blooming Time: June to early July.

Description: Usually an upright shrub up to 8 feet tall with smooth branches. Leaves are opposite on the stems, varied in shape, and have very coarse veins. Upper leaves are elliptical, the lower 3-lobed much like a maple leaf. All are toothed and turn red to maroon in the Fall. The small 5-petaled, white to pinkish flowers are tubular and flare out at the end and are in clusters above the leaves. The soft, translucent, red to orange berries ripen in August and have an unusual odor. A sour berry with a long flat seed that is good for jellies, syrups and catsup.

Comments: Berries are frequently confused with red currants. Berries of the currants hang down in chains, leaves are all maple-leaf shape and are alternate on the stems. See page 77 in Miscellaneous Section.

WILD STRAWBERRY

Fragaria virginiana

Family: Rose / Rosaceae

Habitat: Fields and open slopes at low elevations in Eastern Alaska, and in Interior Alaska (in the Fairbanks area).

Blooming Time: June to early July.

Description: A plant, arising from a thick rootstalk, with 3 coarse, toothed, elongated, pointed leaflets. The white flowers have 5 rounded petals and look like a small garden variety Strawberry. The small red berries ripen in late July and August and are very tasty.

Comments: A similar species, *Fragaria chiloensis*, is found in coastal areas of Southeastern Alaska and in Southcental Alaska and the Aleutian Chain.

BOG CANDLE

Platanthera dilatata

Family: Orchid / Orchidaceae

Habitat: Margins of lakes, wet meadows in Southeastern and coastal Southcentral Alaska, and the Aleutian Chain.

Blooming Time: Late June, July, and early August.

Description: A fleshy plant 10 to 18" tall with long, narrow, pointed, parallel-veined leaves, the lower ones broader. The heavy spike has many small, aromatic flowers with 3 petals and 3 sepals.

Comments: Hybridization is common with the green-flowered, somewhat taller, Fisher Orchid, *Platanthera convallariaefolia*; and the Narrow-leafed Green Orchid, *Platanthera hyperborea*, see page 83 in Miscellaneous Section. All are aromatic. A similar white orchid, Hooded Ladies Tresses, *Spiranthes Romanzoffiana*, has tubular, less-flaring flowers in spirals around the stem.

Bog Candle (Hatcher Pass)

Hooded Ladies Tresses (Hatcher Pass)

LAPLAND DIAPENSIA

Diapensia lapponicum ssp. obovata

Family: Diapensia / Diapensiaceae

Habitat: Tundra and high alpine areas throughout most of Alaska.

Blooming Time: Late May to late June-- soon after snow melts.

Description: A sub-shrub (hugging the ground) with rosettes of tiny, hard, oval, evergreen leaves forming small mounds. The somewhat cup-shaped flowers have 5 rounded petals (sometimes pinkish) and 5 stamens. The seed capsule is divided into 3 parts. The flowers which are about 3/4" across are borne on 1" stems above the leaves.

Comments: Easily distinguished when in bloom; however, leaves are similar to Alpine Azalea, *Loisileuria procumbens,* whose leaves are spread out on long stems, see page 21 in Pink Section.

Lapland Diapensia (Chugach Mts.)

Watermelon Berry (Anchorage)

Watermelon Berry (Anchorage)

False Solomon's Seal (Eklutna)

WATERMELON BERRY, TWISTED STALK, WILD CUCUMBER

Streptopus amplexifolius
Family: Lily / Liliaceae
Habitat: Moist woods and meadows throughout Southeastern, Central, Southcentral, and Western Alaska, and the Aleutian Chain.
Blooming Time: Mid-June to late July.
Description: A tall (1-1/2 to 4 foot) branched, perennial plant with many smooth, rather thin, alternate leaves on the crooked (somewhat zigzag) stem. Leaves have parallel veins, are ovate to lanceolate, have an acute tip, are entire in the margin, and clasp the stem. The young shoots (in Spring) are eaten raw and taste like cucumber. The lower stems are covered with fine, dark hairs. The flowers are on a twisted stem and are attached to the under side of the leaf at its base. The flowers have 6 white to cream-colored tepals that are reflexed. In August, they produce a red, oval berry with many seeds.
Comments: The sweet, juicy berries are used for jellies and syrups. The new shoots, younger leaves and flower buds are tasty additions to salads. The zigzag stem, twisted flower stalk, and characteristic hairs on the lower stems help to differentiate it from the toxic False Solomon's Seal (see below).

FALSE SOLOMON'S SEAL

Smilacina stellata
Family: Lily / Liliaceae
Habitat: Meadows and damp, sub-alpine slopes in the Cook Inlet area.
Blooming Time: Late May to late June.
Description: A perennial plant (6 to 24" tall) with alternate leaves growing from horizontal roots. Leaves are long. oblanceolate, sessile, entire, have parallel veins, and usually angle upwards on the stiff upright stem. Flowers are in a short raceme at the ends of the stems, and have 6 pointed, white tepals. Fruit is 3-parted, dark red with 3 large seeds.
Comments: Poisonous. Take care not to confuse with the Spring shoots of Watermelon Berry. False Solomon's seal is bitter and has no black hairs on stem.

MISCELLANEOUS PLANTS AND TREES

Woodlands, Matanuska Valley
Yellow Spotted Ladyslipper, Dogwood, Star Flower

Chocolate Lily (Chugach Mts.)

CHOCOLATE LILY, KAMCHATKA FRITILLARY, RICE LILY

Fritillaria camschatcensis

Family: Lily / Liliaceae

Habitat: Damp, woodlands and meadows throughout Southeastern, Southcentral Alaska and the Aleutian Chain.

Blooming Time: Mid-June to mid-July.

Description: A very variable (according to habitat) perennial plant, 5 to 18" tall, arising from a white bulb. It multiplies by tiny rice-like bulblets that form around it. Seedlings have 1 elongated leaf. In subsequent years, it develops 1 or 2 more single leaves; and, finally, whorls of leaves. Flower stems arise from the leaf whorls and have 3 brown petals and 3 greenish-brown sepals (appearing like 6 petals).

Comments: The immature seeds as well as the bulbs are edible raw or cooked. Due to the unpleasant aroma of the flowers, it has also been nicknamed; Skunk Lily and Outhouse Lily. Seed pods are large, erect and are divided into 6 sections. This is a distinctive plant because of its growth and brown flowers.

Marsh Cinquefoil (Anchorage)

MARSH CINQUEFOIL, MARSH FIVEFINGER

Potentilla palustris

Family: Rose / Rosaceae

Habitat: Very wet meadows, marshes, in shallow water, and along streams throughout Alaska.

Blooming Time: July.

Description: A sprawling plant (up to 2 feet) which has a somewhat woody, creeping rootstalk. The stipulate, toothed leaves are somewhat palmate and have 5 to 7 separate leaflets. The purplish-brown, 5-petaled, pointed flowers are distinctive. After blooming, the sepals fold up over the ovary; a characteristic of *Potentillas*.

NORTHERN RED CURRANT

Ribes triste

Family: Gooseberry / Grossulariaceae

Habitat: Moist woods and meadows up to timberline throughout most of Alaska, except the North Slope, Aleutian Chain, coastal Western Alaska and most of Southeastern Alaska.

Blooming Time: Mid-May to mid-June.

Description: A shrub with shredding bark usually upright; but, occasionally, sprawling (2 to 3 feet). Leaves are toothed and 3 to 5-lobed (maple shaped). They are arranged alternately on the branches and turn red in the Fall. The small, brick red flowers are on weak, drooping stems hanging under the leaves. The tasty berries which ripen in July are red and translucent.

Comments: There are many varieties of Currants in Alaska. All except Northern Black Currant, *Ribes hudsonium* (which has white flowers) have berries on long, drooping stems. All are edible and all have "maple shaped" leaves. The Bristly Black Currant or Gooseberry, *Ribes lacustre*, has very small leaves, thorns, and hairy black berries. Trailing Black Currant, *Ribes laxiflorum*, has blue to black berries with hairs.

Northern Red Currant (Anchorage)

Northern Red Currant (Anchorage)

TIMBERBERRY, NORTHERN COMANDRA, PUMPKIN BERRY

Geocaulon lividum

Family: Sandlewood / Santalaceae

Habitat: Dry places, usually open woods in Eastern, Interior, Southcentral and Western Alaska, except coastal areas.

Blooming Time: Very early. Mid to late May.

Description: An upright plant with alternate, oval leaves on a 3 to 6" stem, arising from a horizontal root. The tiny green flowers with 5 sepals produce orange berries in the Fall.

Comments: This plant is considered to be semi-parasitic, and often the leaves are mottled with brown. The berries are edible, but not very tasty.

Timberberry (Anchorage)

Soapberry (Glenn Hwy.)

Soapberry (Glenn Hwy.)

Sidebells Pyrola (Kenai Peninsula)

SOAPBERRY

Shepherdia canadensis

Family: Oleaster / Elaeagnaceae

Habitat: Dry, sandy, sunny areas or open woodlands throughout most of Alaska, except coastal areas.

Blooming Time: May.

Description: A deciduous shrub up to 3 feet tall, having distinctive, scurfy, brownish scales (like sandpaper) on young twigs, underside of leaves and sepals. This causes the new buds in Spring to look copper colored. The leaves, which start appearing with the early blooms, are ovate, green above and whitish beneath, with the brown scales. Flowers are salverform, yellowish, very small, have 4 sepals and are sessile. They produce small, edible, oval, red, bitter, translucent berries in August. Male and female flowers are borne on separate bushes.

Comments: Indians used the sweetened, whipped berries as a dessert topping, and the berries are a favorite food of bears. Very common in dry, rocky areas along Turnagain Arm, the Glenn Highway from Palmer to Glenallen, and the Denali Park area. It is found throughout Eastern, Interior and Southcentral Alaska.

Female
flower

Male
flower

SIDEBELLS PYROLA

Pyrola secunda

Family: Wintergreen / Pyrolaceae

Habitat: Woods in Southeastern, Southcentral, Eastern and Interior Alaska and Kodiak Island.

Blooming Time: Late June to early July.

Description: A low evergreen plant with yellowish-green ovate, glabrous leaves, arising from a long creeping root. The small, green, bell-shaped flowers usually hang on one side of the slightly curved 3 to 5" stem. They have a protruding style and the seed heads are distinctive.

DEVIL'S CLUB

Echinopanax horridum

Family: Ginseng / Araliaceae

Habitat: Moist coastal areas of Southcentral Alaska, Cook Inlet, Kodiak Island, and Southeastern Alaska.

Blooming Time: June.

Description: A shrub, 4 to 8 feet tall, that forms dense thickets that are difficult to penetrate. The very large "maple-shaped" leaves have spines on their veins and stems. The greenish flowers are on a dense spiny woody spike and are followed, in August, by small reddish berries that also have thorns. In winter they frequently have just 1 or 2 spiny club-like spikes left.

Devil's club (Anchorage)

Comments: The berries are considered toxic. This shrub forms dense thickets in moist woods. Homesteaders who obtained property containing the plant discovered that they had very rich soil (once they conquered clearing the land). Extracts and poultices of this plant have been used extensively as medicines by the natives of Southeastern Alaska for many illnesses and infections. It is closely related to Ginseng.

RUSTY MENZIESIA, FOOL'S HUCKLEBERRY, FALSE AZALEA

Menziesia ferruginea

Family: Heath / Ericaceae

Habitat: Moist woods in Southeastern and Southcentral Alaska.

Blooming Time: June.

Description: An erect shrub with light brown branches that have somewhat shredding bark. The thin light-bluish green ovate leaves have a slightly wavy margin. The flowers are bell-shaped and light orange to rust colored. The star-shaped seed pods are distinctive.

Devil's Club in Winter (Anchorage)

Comments: The leaves form from a central point, much like Azaleas. The bell-shaped flowers can be mistaken for Blueberry flowers by novices, who may return to an area in August looking for berries. Hence the name, "Fool's Huckleberry".

Rusty Menziesia (Anchorage)

Western Columbine (Chugach Mts.)

WESTERN COLUMBINE
Aquilegia formosa

Family: Buttercup or Crowfoot / Ranunculaceae

Habitat: Wooded mountain slopes and meadows in Southeastern and coastal Southcentral Alaska.

Blooming Time: Mid-June through July.

Description: A branched perennial plant up to 30" tall. The basal leaves are twice divided into 3 parts with rounded shallow lobes. Stem leaves are divided once. Leaves are dark green above and grayish-green below. Flowers are large (1 to 1-1/2"), have 5 red sepals with spurs, yellow tubular petals and protruding stamens.

Comments: Another species, Blue Columbine, *Aquilegia brevistylla* is found in Eastern and Southcentral Alaska and the Yukon Territory. It is a shorter plant with smaller lavender and white flowers.

Roseroot (Chugach Mts.)

ROSEROOT, ROSEWORT, KING'S CROWN
Sedum rosea

Family: Stonecrop / Crassulaceae

Habitat: Rocky places and alpine slopes throughout most of Alaska.

Blooming Time: June.

Description: A fleshy plant with slightly toothed, crowded, glabrous, bluish-green leaves on heavy stems topped by a cluster of small dark reddish (occasionally yellow) 4 or 5-petalled flowers. The heavy root, when cut, smells somewhat like roses.

Comments: The young plants may be eaten raw or cooked. This plant is very variable depending upon elevation and habitat. In the Denali Park area, you may see very dwarfed specimens as yet not classified as a separate sub-species. Its leaves are smaller, darker green and the flower color is more intense.

ARCTIC DOCK

Rumex arcticus

Family: Buckwheat / Polygonaceae

Habitat: Wet places throughout most of Alaska.

Blooming Time: July and August.

Description: A large (up to 4 foot tall) heavy-stalked plant with large, glabrous, lance-shaped leaves. Most leaves are on the flowering stalk and are reduced in size as they grow upwards. The tiny flowers, which have no petals, have large, colorful red or green bracts beneath them on the branched colorful stalk.

Comments: Many varieties of Dock are found in Alaska with variances of leaf size and shape. All have edible leaves and taste slightly sour, as they are related to Rhubarb. The flower stalks may be dried for use in floral arrangements.

Arctic Dock (Glenn Hwy.)

Sheep Sorrel

MOUNTAIN SORREL

Oxyria digyna

Family: Buckwheat / Polygonaceae

Habitat: Alpine meadows and wet places in the mountains throughout Alaska.

Blooming Time: July.

Description: Long-stemmed, glabrous, kidney-shaped leaves surround a 6 to 10" tall flowering stalk of tiny flowers with reddish bracts.

Comments: These tasty leaves are refreshing to chew on while hiking in the mountains. Another common similar species, Sheep Sorrel, *Rumex acetosella*, with arrow-shaped leaves has been introduced in yards, roadsides, etc. and may be eaten in the same way. See drawing above.

Mountain Sorrel (Chugach Mts.)

False Hellebore, new shoots (Chugach Mts.)

False Hellebore (Hatcher Pass)

Prairie Sagebrush (Bison Gulch)

FALSE HELLEBORE

Veratrum viride

Family: Lily / Liliaceae

Habitat: Meadows in Southeastern and Southcentral Alaska, Kodiak Island and the Cook Inlet area.

Blooming Time: July and August.

Description: A large plant (up to 5' tall) with very large broadly ovate leaves, with obvious linear veins, that clasp the thick stalk. The tall flowering stalk has branched drooping stems of numerous green flowers with 6 tepals (3 petals & sepals that look alike).

Comments: This is a very poisonous plant that, if eaten, may cause vomiting, paralysis, and death. The new shoots could easily be mistaken for the edible wild cucumber, especially by the novice. See page 74 in White Section.

PRAIRIE SAGEBRUSH, FRIGID WORMWOOD

Artemisia frigida

Family: Aster / Asteraceae

Habitat: Dry, rocky, open, well-drained slopes throughout most of Interior Alaska and the northern part of Southcentral Alaska.

Blooming Time: June and July.

Description: A low plant (6 to 14") having a woody base with finely divided, silvery, and silky leaves that are 2 to 3 times divided and strongly aromatic (like sage). The flowers which are on upright stems, are inconspicuous, nodding and look like the center of a daisy.

Comments: It may be used as a seasoning. There are several, low-growing Artemisias in Alaska. All are somewhat aromatic and most have silvery-looking leaves. *Artemisia arctica* is an exception, with bright green, toothed, slightly broader leaves. It is very common on alpine slopes, tundra, and sometimes in lower elevations throughout most of Alaska.

NORTHERN GREEN BOG ORCHID

Platanthera hyperborea

Family: Orchis / Orchidaceae

Habitat: Wet meadows, bogs, along streams from sea level to treeline in Eastern, Central and Southcentral Alaska.

Blooming Time: July.

Description: Upright, heavy, fleshy stems (8 to 14") with long, narrow leaves with linear veins. The small, yellowish-green, sweet scented flowers with 3 petals and 3 sepals cover most of the heavy stems.

Comments: These plants hybridize easily with Bog Candle, *Platanthera dilatata,* see page 73 in White Section. *Platanthera convallariaefolia* is a taller plant with larger leaves and heavier darker green flower spike. There are 2 *Listera* species (Twayblade) which have opposite leaves and flowers with a large triangular lower petal. They are 4 to 8" tall, and have several flowers on a stem.

Northern Green Bog Orchid (Hatcher Pass)

COMMON WORMWOOD

Artemisia Tilesii

Family: Aster / Asteraceae

Habitat: Open woodlands in low elevations and sandy places in low mountainous areas throughout most of the state.

Blooming Time: July and August.

Description: A tall plant (2 to 5 feet) with many branched flower spikes with nodding greenish-yellow flowers that look like the center of a daisy. The leafy plant has deeply cut 3-5 lobed leaves that are smooth and green on top and silvery and hairy beneath.

Comments: There are 4 varieties in Alaska. They are used in dried flowers arrangements and also as additions to salves and bath water as they are very aromatic.

Common Wormwood (Palmer)

Squirrel Tail Grass (Alaska Hwy.)

SQUIRRELTAIL GRASS

Hordeum jubatum

Family: Grass / Poaceae

Habitat: Sandy or gravelly soil throughout most of Alaska, except coastal areas.

Blooming Time: July and August.

Description: A distinctive, showy, annual grass seen introduced along many roadsides. It is 10 to 16" tall, and has large rose to purple flowering spikes.

Comments: Although beautiful, this grass bears caution if you have pets, as the spiked seeds can lodge in their throat and require medical attention.

Broomrape

BROOMRAPE, GROUND CONE

Boschniakia rossica

Family: Broomrape / Orobanchaceae

Habitat: A parasite growing on the roots of <u>only</u> Mountain Alder, *Alnus crispa*, throughout most of Alaska.

Blooming Time: Late June and July.

Description: The tiny reddish-brown flowers grow on a heavy fleshy spike between glabrous brownish bracts. At maturity, the plant is 8 to 12" tall and looks very much like an erect tall soft pine cone. It can be seen, dried and still standing, in the Winter and early Spring.

CROWBERRY, MOSSBERRY

Empetrum nigrum

Family: Crowberry/Empetraceae

Habitat: Woods, heaths, bogs, and alpine slopes (especially north-facing) throughout Alaska.

Blooming Time: May and early June.

Description: A low, mat-forming, evergreen shrub with small, narrow, needle-like leaves. The shrub looks wine or maroon colored early in the season. The early blooming (often as the snow melts) flowers are small, maroon colored, 3-parted, inconspicuous. They are followed by firm, round, black, juicy (but seedy), edible berries.

Crowberry (Chugach Mts.)

Comments: The berries are also called Blackberry by some ethnic groups. The berries may be used for jelly or pies. They are easy to pick, and they keep well.

SHORT-STALK SEDGE

Carex microchaeta

Family: Sedge / Cyperaceae

Crowberry (Chugach Mts.)

Habitat: Tundra, meadows and alpine slopes throughout much of Alaska, except coastal areas.

Blooming Time: July and August.

Description: A 5 to 10" tall plant with many linear basal leaves and obvious old dead stubbles. The flowering spikes are large for the plant and stamens are very showy. The top 1 or 2 are staminate; the lower ones pistillate, drooping when mature. There are many Sedges in Alaska, and it is a complex genus. This species is very common, and showy for its size. It is usually taller than other plants growing in the same area.

Short-stalk Sedge (Chugach Mts.)

Club Moss (Anchorage)

Creeping Jenny (Anchorage)

CLUB MOSS

Lycopodium annotinum

Family: Club Moss / Lycopodiaceae

Habitat: Woodlands and low alpine slopes throughout most of Alaska.

Blooming Time: No "blooms". Spore producing plant.

Description: A low (4 to 7") creeping, evergreen plant with stiff needle-like yellowish-green leaves bearing spikes of fine spores.

Comments: The spores readily ignite and were used as the flashpowder of early day photographers. There are several varieties of Club Moss in Alaska and they are common in woodlands. Most have spike-like branches; except for Ground Pine or Tree Club Moss, *Lycopodium obscurum*, which looks like miniature pine trees; and, Christmas Greens or Creeping Jenny, *Lycopodium complanatum*,which has branched flat (cedar like) leaves. This variety has been commonly used like a rope to bind together other evergreens for Christmas wreaths.

STRAWBERRY SPINACH, STRAWBERRY BLITE

Chenopodium capitatum

Family: Goosefoot / Chenopodiaceae

Habitat: Dry soil, waste places and roadsides in Central Alaska, Eastern Alaska, and interior portion of Southcentral Alaska.

Blooming Time: Bloom-July. Fruit-July and August.

Description: An upright (decumbent in fruit) annual with triangular, glabrous leaves with wavy edges. The flowers are very tiny and inconspicuous, but followed by showy, bunched, round, reddish fruits.

Comments: The sweet, edible fruit may be eaten raw or used for jelly and syrup. The tasty leaves are very similar to its close relative, Spinach.

Strawberry Spinach (Alaska Highway)

HORSETAIL

Equisetum arvense

Family: Horsetail / Equisetaceae

Habitat: A variety of different habitats, elevations and soil conditions throughout Alaska.

Blooming Time: Spring.

Description: Hollow stems with vertical ridges. Very narrow, rough feeling, leaves in whorls at joints on the stems. Spreads rapidly by horizontal roots, frequently forming lacy (somewhat ferny) carpets in moist woodlands. The spore-bearing Spring phase dies down after production, and is replaced by the vegetative or leafy phase.

Comments: The plant is used as an abrasive cleaner for pots and pans as it contains silica. The peeled inner portion of the "Spring Phase" is tasty. There are several varieties of Horsetail in Alaska. Some produce spore-bearing portion at the end of the vegetative stem. In some varieties, the leaves are very short, almost non-existant. Do not confuse with Mares Tail, *Hippuris vulgaris*, which is a flower-producing water plant that looks like narrow miniature Spruce trees.

Horsetail, spore bearing Spring Phase (Anchorage)

Horsetail, vegetative phase (Anchorage)

LYME GRASS, BEACH RYE GRASS

Elymus arenarius

Family: Grass / Poaceae

Habitat: Sandy beaches and mouths of rivers in coastal areas of Alaska.

Blooming Time: July and August.

Description: A tall (2 to 5'), native grass with long, wide, flat, bluish-green leaves and tall, stiff, heavy flower spikes that are very attractive in dried flower arrangements.

Comments: This has also been introduced along roadsides in some areas and does well under these conditions. This grass is commonly used to weave grass baskets.

Lyme Grass (Homer)

Alaska Willow catkins (Denali Hwy.)

ALASKA WILLOW, FELT LEAF WILLOW

Salix alaxensis

Family: Willow / Salicaceae

Habitat: Sub-alpine and low alpine slopes, often near streams, throughout most of Alaska.

Blooming Time: Late May through early June.

Description: A tall shrub or tree (15 to 25') with young twigs that are distinctly white and wooly in the winter and early spring. The oblanceolate (oval & pointed) leaves are densely covered with white hairs on the underside. The catkins are very long and upright.

Comments: This is one of the minor producers of "Diamond Willow" in Alaska. Diamond Willow develops, in wet areas, when a fungus attacks a broken off branch area. Eventually, the fungus eats diamond-shaped areas into the trunk. The wood is highly prized by craftspeople. It is stripped of its bark, and carved into lamp posts, canes and other hand-crafted items. The major producer of Diamond Willow is Bebb Willow, *Salix depressa*. Another interesting willow is Barclay's Willow, *Salix Barclayi*. It is sometimes attacked by an insect infestation which causes the leaves to become deformed into "roses" at the ends of the branches.

Young buds and inner bark of willow are eaten raw and are a favorite food of natives. Willows contain salicin, so chewing on leaves or young twigs can be an emergency medicine for headaches. It is apparent from observing moose browsing areas that some varieties are more bitter than others. There are about 30 varieties of upright shrubby willows in Alaska.

Bebb Willow, showing diamonds (Glenallen)

Barclay's Willow, showing "roses"   M.Barker

ROUND-LEAF WILLOW

Salix rotundifolia

Family: Willow / Salicaceae

Habitat: Tundra and rocky alpine areas throughout most of Alaska.

Blooming Time: Late May to late June.

Description: Dwarf, mat-forming shrub with very small, round, shiny leaves. Catkins are very short and reddish. One of the smallest of the willows.

Comments: Another common small willow is Skeleton leaf Willow, *Salix phlebophylla*, which has small, oval and pointed leaves with prominent veins that remain intact at the end of the season giving it a "skeleton leaf" effect.

Round-leaf Willow (Hatcher Pass)

Arctic Willow (Denali Park)

Ernie Fish

ARCTIC WILLOW

Salix arctica

Family: Willow / Salicaceae

Habitat: Tundra, heaths and alpine ridges throughout Alaska.

Blooming Time: May and early June.

Description: A common spreading dwarf shrub with thick branches hugging the rocky ground. The round (very variable) leaves are dark green above; pale and somewhat hairy below. Catkins are frequently very reddish.

Comments: Willows hybridize very easily, making identification quite difficult.

Dwarf Willow Catkins (Bison Gulch)

Wood Fern (Anchorage)

Lady Fern (Hatcher Pass)

Ostrich Fern (Anchorage)

WOOD FERN

Dryopteris dilatata

Family: Shield Fern / Aspidaceae

Habitat: Moist woods and meadows throughout Alaska, except Eastern Alaska, the Brooks Range and North Slope.

Blooming Time: There are no "blooms". Spores are visible on the underside of leaves by mid-Summer.

Description: A tall fern (up to 2') arising from a stout, coarse rootstalk covered with bases of old stipes. Stipes are covered with course brown scales. Leaflets start about halfway up the stipe; starting broad and tapering to a point at the end.

Comments: The curled fronds ("fiddleheads", the early Spring growth form) are edible; but, best if the brown scales are rubbed off. This should be done when they are dry.

A similar looking fern is Lady Fern, *Athyrium filix-femina*, which grows 2 to 4' tall in the southern half of the State. Leaflets start small near the base of the stipe, are longer in the middle, and then taper to a point at the end. Spores are produced on the under sides of the leaves.

OSTRICH FERN

Matteuccia struthiopteris

Family: Lady Fern / Athyriaceae

Habitat: Very wet woods (at low elevations) especially along streams in a few isolated areas---Fairbanks, Valdez, the Matanuska and Susitna Valleys.

Blooming Time: No blooms. This plant produces spores on a separate "leaflike" fertile frond.

Description: A clump fern with fronds (1-1/2 to 3' tall) growing in a funnel-like form. Leaflets start small near the base, become wide in the middle, then narrowing to a point at the tip. The leaf-like fertile frond of this large fern helps in identification.

Comments: The lack of scales on the fiddleheads of this fern make it a tasty vegetable, cooked briefly like asparagus. Ferns are also tasty raw, but should be eaten in moderation.

FRAGRANT SHIELD FERN

Dryopteris fragrans

Family: Shield Fern / Aspidiaceae

Habitat: Open, dry, rocky outcroppings throughout most of Alaska; except the Aleutian Chain, Southeastern, coastal areas of Southcentral and Southwestern Alaska, and the Arctic Coast.

Blooming Time: No "blooms". Spore bearing on the underside of leaves.

Description: A small (up to 8") clump fern with many stiff, coarse-looking leaf blades and many old reddish-brown, curled fronds and stipes arising from a thick rootstalk.

Fragrant Shield Fern (Turnagain Arm)

Comments: Neither the author nor her friends have been able to ascertain how this plant received its name, as it seems to have no obvious aroma.

FRAGILE FERN

Cystopteris fragilis

Family: Lady Fern / Athyriaceae

Habitat: Rocky places in woods, clearings, and in the mountains throughout most of Alaska, except the Arctic Coast.

Blooming Time: No "blooms". Spore bearing on the underside of leaves.

Description: A small (up to 7") delicate fern in small groupings, spreading by underground rhizomes.

Fragile Fern (Turnagain Arm)

PARSLEY FERN

Cryptogramma crispa

Family: Mountain Parsley / Cryptogrammaceae

Habitat: Rocky areas on the Aleutian Chain, Southeastern and Southcentral Alaska, and the southern portion of Interior Alaska.

Blooming Time: No "blooms". Spore bearing plant with separate fertile frond standing up above the foliage.

Description: A small (up to 6"), loose, clump plant from a heavy rootstalk with remnants of old stipes. Leaf sections are finely dissected, much like leaf sections of common Parsley. Old dried leaves are common around the base of the plant.

Parsley Fern (Turnagain Arm)

DECIDUOUS TREES

Black Cottonwood---*Populus trichocarpa*
Balsam Poplar---*Populus balsamifera*

Very large trees (40 to 90') with deeply grooved, thick bark; young trees have smooth bark. Leaf shape is very variable. Young trees often have very large leaves. Most are large pointed, elongated, heart-shaped leaves that turn bright yellow in the Fall. Balsam Poplar is found throughout Alaska, and Black Cottonwood in Southeastern and Southcentral Alaska. Hybridization occurs where ranges overlap. They are common near rivers and near stream beds up into the mountains. The bark is used by craftsman for paintings and woodcarvings.

Quaking Aspen---*Populus tremuloides*

A medium sized, short lived, tree (18 to 40') with smooth, greenish-gray bark becoming grooved near the base on older trees. The broad, sharply-pointed, heart-shaped leaves tremble with the slightest breeze, due the long delicate petioles. It is found throughout most of Interior and Southcentral Alaska. The leaves turn bright yellow in the Fall. They prefer dry, sandy or rocky ground from lowlands up to alpine. They often look misshapen or gnarled, especially in exposed sites.

Paper Birch---*Betula papyrifera*

A medium sized tree (up to 50') with whitish, peeling bark and horizontal markings. The coarse-veined, sharply-toothed, pointed, heart-shaped leaves turn yellow in the Fall. They are common throughout Alaska at all elevations, except extreme coastal areas. They hybridize with Kenai River Birch, *Betula Kenaica,* (which has reddish bark) where their ranges overlap. Dwarf Birch, *Betula nana*, shrubs with small, round, toothed leaves turn reddish-orange in the Fall and are particularly visible in and near Denali Park. Birches produce Salicin, a bitter chemical related to Aspirin, in their bark. This discourages moose from browsing them too heavily. Young trees produce more than older trees, whose branches are out of reach of the browsing animals.

Larch / Tamarack---*Larix laricina*

A small tree (up to 30') found in bogs in Interior Alaska. The short needles, which grow in clusters, are deciduous, so fall off in the Fall.

Willows---*Salix sp.*

There are several Willows in Alaska that grow to tree size, but most still grow in clumps. Most have ovate to elliptical leaves. All produce catkins, and contain Salicin in varying amounts.

Balsam Poplar (Parks Hwy.)

Black Cottonwood in Winter
(Anchorage)

Birch (Matanuska Valley)

Larch (Fairbanks)

Quaking Aspen (Copper Center)

EVERGREEN TREES

Black Spruce---*Picea mariana*

Small tree (up to 30 feet) found in bogs or wet areas at low elevations throughout Interior Alaska and the Cook Inlet area of Southcentral Alaska. Young branches have rusty-colored hairs. Needles are 4-angled with stomata on all sides, and are short (1/4 to 1/2"). The small, 3/4 to 1-1/4", egg-shaped cones, which grow close to the main trunk, remain on the trees for years, usually waiting for the heat of a forest fire to release the seeds. Due to a high water table and poor growing conditions, these trees are often very deformed. They often hybridize with White Spruce and, occasionally, Sitka Spruce.

White Spruce---*Picea glauca*

A medium tree (30 to 75') found in woodlands and into alpine throughout most of the State. Hybridization with other Spruce species is common. Needles are 3/8 to 3/4" long and are 4-angled with stomata on all sides, and have a skunky smell. The medium sized (1-1/4 to 2") elongated cones, which grow on the outer branches, fall off each Spring. Alpine specimens often are stunted, and sometimes resemble Junipers.

Sitka Spruce---*Picea sitchensis* (The Alaska State Tree)

A tall tree (100 to 200') found in coastal areas of Southcentral and Southeastern Alaska. Needles are 3/4 to 1-1/8" long and slightly flattened with stomata only on the underside and slightly keeled at the ends. Branches tend to droop more than White Spruce. The large, long (2 to 3-1/2") cones have rippled bracts and fall off each Spring.

Mountain Hemlock---*Tsuga mertensiana*
Western Hemlock---*Tsuga heterophylla*

These trees have flat needles and small cones, and are found in coastal areas and moist mountain ridges. In windswept mountain areas, Mountain Hemlock becomes very dwarfed and misshapen. Mountain Hemlock has long cones, 1 to 1-1/2", Western Hemlock cones are usually only 1/2 to 1" long.

Sitka Spruce (Seward Hwy.)

Mountain Hemlock (Chugach Mts.)

PLANT FAMILY CHARACTERISTICS

Plants are divided into families by differences of reproductive parts; such as, number and placement of stamens, how the ovaries are divided, placement of seeds within the ovaries, manner of seed disbursement, etc. However, these characteristics are not always available nor easily noticed, so I have listed below some other, more obvious, characteristics to look for. In botany, there are a lot of "usually"s, some families vary greatly, and many oddities do occur. The characteristics listed are aimed at our Alaskan genera only.

(1) Aster / Asteraceae---formerly the daisy or Composite/ Compositae. Herbaceous plants or shrubs having a head of flowers (composed of many flowers), usually disk flowers, surrounded by showy ray flowers (sometimes incorrectly called petals) with a circle of bracts at the base. Leaf shape and placement variable according to genus.

(2) Bladderwort / Lentibulareaceae---insectivorous plants of wet areas having a short spike of irregularly shaped flowers with 2 to 5 sepals, 5 united petals, and 2 stamens. Terrestrial plants have a rosette of leaves, while aquatic varieties have finely dissected leaves on long, floating stems. Since these plants are generally not seen, they are not shown in this book.

(3) Bluebell / Campanulaceae---herbaceous plants with a few flowers having 5 sepals, 5 petals (united at base and, frequently, bell-shaped), 5 stamens, and 1 ovary. Leaves are simple and alternate on stems.

(4) Borage / Boraginaceae---herbaceous plants with branched stems with many flowers having 5 united sepals, 5 united petals (bell-shaped or salverform), 5 stamens, and an ovary divided into 2 parts (often times lobed, giving the appearance of 4 parts). Leaves are alternate, simple, often hairy and frequently buds are in a curled cyme.

(5) Buckwheat / Polygonaceae---herbaceous plants with a spike of many small flowers having 5 sepals, no petals; and, usually, 8 stamens. Leaves are simple, sometimes basal. but usually on the stem.

(6) Buttercup or Crowfoot / Ranunculaceae---herbaceous plants with 1 to many common flowers usually having 5 sepals, 5 petals, many stamens (tight cushion effect) divided into 1 to many sections. (this is a very variable family having unusual numbers of petals; and, sometimes completely lacking petals). Leaves are frequently divided into a lobed or dissected crowfoot (birdfoot) pattern, have long stems, and are predominantly basal. Some genera do not have petals and the number of sepals is variable. Many members of this family are poisonous.

(7) Calla / Araceae---herbaceous plants having large, simple leaves and a large floral type leaf below a spike of inconspicuous flowers having no petals and 6 stamens. The fruit is a berry, frequently poisonous.

(8) Crowberry / Empetrum--------evergreen shrubs having inconspicuous flowers of 3 bracts, 3 to 6 sepals (sometimes in whorls and confused as petals) and 2 to 4 stamens. The ovary is divided into many parts and produces a round, black berry. Leaves are simple and heath-like.

(9) Diapensia / Diapensiaceae---evergreen shrubs having flowers with 5 sepals, 5 united petals, 5 stamens, and the ovary divided into 3 sections. Leaves are very small. There is one alpine member in Alaska.

(10) Dogwood / Cornaceae---shrubs having clusters of very small flowers consisting of 4 showy bracts, 4 sepals, 4 petals, 4 stamens, and 1 ovary which produces a soft, inedible berry. The 4 large, showy bracts are often confused with petals. The simple leaves have arcuate veins.

(11) Earthsmoke / Fumariaceae---herbaceous plants having delicately branched stems of small, irregular flowers having 2 sepals, 4 united petals (forming a spur), 6 stamens, and 1 ovary. Most leaves are basal and are finely dissected. The stems are very soft and watery.

(12) Evening Primrose / Onagraceae---herbaceous plants having spikes of showy flowers with 4 sepals, 4 petals, and an ovary seen distinctly as a branched stigma. Leaves are simple and on the stems, arising from deep horizontal roots.

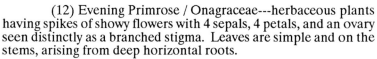

(13) Figwort or Snapdragon / Scrophulariaceae---herbaceous plants with spikes or racemes or many irregularly shaped flowers having 5 united sepals, 5 united petals, 4 (sometimes 2) stamens, and 1 ovary. Most leaves are simple, except for Pedicularis, which is pinnately divided.

(14) Flax / Linaceae---herbaceous plants with simple stem leaves. Common flowers having 5 sepals, 5 petals, and 5 stamens. The one member in Alaska has blue petals.

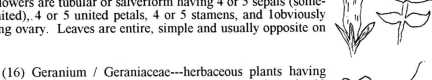

(15) Gentian / Gentianaceae---herbaceous plants with stiff stems. Flowers are tubular or salverform having 4 or 5 sepals (sometimes united), 4 or 5 united petals, 4 or 5 stamens, and 1 obviously protruding ovary. Leaves are entire, simple and usually opposite on stems.

(16) Geranium / Geraniaceae---herbaceous plants having branched stems of large flowers with 5 sepals, 5 clawed petals, 10 stamens, and a 5-parted extruded ovary that resembles a Crane's bill. Alaska members have long-stemmed, palmately-divided leaves, mostly basal.

(17) Ginseng / Araliaceae---spiny shrubs with a raceme of umbels of very small flowers having 5 sepals, 5 petals, 5 stamens, and 1 ovary that forms a berry. Very large maple-like, palmate leaves.

(18) Gooseberry / Grossulariaceae---shrubs sometimes with thorns, having small flowers with 4 or 5 sepals, 5 very small petals, 5 stamens, and a 2-parted ovary in the form of a berry. Leaves are usually lobed with teeth.

(19) Goosefoot / Chenopodiaceae---herbaceous plants with spikes of small, mostly green, inconspicuous clusters of flowers with 5 sepals, no petals, 5 stamens, and 1 ovary. These are mostly weedy plants usually with opposite leaves.

(20) Heath / Ericaceae---mostly shrubs, frequently evergreen, and often with bell or urn-shaped flowers. Flowers have 4 or 5 (sometimes united) sepals, 4 or 5 (usually united) petals, 4 or 5 stamens, and 1 ovary. The leaves are usually entire, simple and often narrow.

(21) Honeysuckle / Caprifoliaceae---shrubs with tubular or salverform flowers having 5 sepals, 5 united petals, 5 stamens, and 1 ovary. Leaves are toothed and opposite.

(22) Iris / Iridaceae---herbaceous plants growing from rhizomes and having stout stems. Flowers have 3 sepals, 3 petals, 3 stamens, and a 3-parted ovary. Leaves are long and blade-like with linear (parallel) veins.

(23) Lily / Liliaceae---frequently bulbous plants usually with a stout flower stalk. Flowers have 6 tepals (3 sepals, 3 petals), 6 stamens, and a 3-parted ovary. Flowers are in a raceme or umbel. Leaves have parallel veins and, frequently, clasp the stem.

(24) Mustard / Brassicaceae---herbaceous plants with branched inflorescences of flowers having 4 sepals, 4 petals, 6 stamens (4 high and 2 low), and 1 ovary. Leaves frequently are basal but can continue up the flower stalk. Distinct seed stalk as silicle or silique. Most members have edible leaves.

(25) Madder / Rubiaceae---herbaceous plants having a panicle of small salverform flowers with 4 sepals, 4 united petals, 4 stamens, and 1 2-parted ovary. Some varieties have square stems, all have entire leaves that are opposite of in a whorl.

(26) Mint / Menthaceae---herbaceous plants with irregular flowers with 4 united petals, (a 2-lobed upper lip, and 3 petals joined as a lower lip). Stems are usually square; leaves are opposite, simple and toothed. Most Alaskan species have been introduced. None are pictured in this book. Our native species has lavender flowers and is found in wet places.

(27) Moschatel / Adoxaceae---herbaceous plants. There is one small member in Alaska having one 4-petalled flower at the end of the stem and four 5-petalled flowers surrounding it. The basal leaves are thin, yellowish-green with broad, toothed lobes. Blooms very early and is very small. (Not pictured in this book.)

(28) Nettle / Urticaceae---herbaceous upright plants having limp spikes of inconspicuous flowers. Leaves are opposite, and stems sometimes square. Plants are often equipped with stinging hairs.

(29) Oleaster / Elaeagnaceae---shrubs having salverform flowers with 4 sepals, no petals, 4 stamens, and 1 ovary in the form of a berry. Leaves are simple, entire, and have scales.

(30) Orchid / Orchidaceae---herbaceous plants with irregularly shaped flowers having 3 sepals, 3 petals (the lower are "sac-like"). Flower stalks are stout, leaves usually alternate (sometimes opposite), simple with parallel veins (monocot).

(31) Parsley / Apiaceae---herbaceous plants with umbels of small flowers having 5 sepals, 5 petals, 5 stamens, and a 2-parted ovary. Most leaves are pinnately divided and finely dissected or toothed. Some plants have hollow stems and leaves with petioles that clasp the stems.

(32) Pea / Fabaceae---herbaceous plants having irregular flowers, with 5 united sepals, 5 petals (the lower 2 joined to form a keel), 10 stamens, and 1 pistil. Leaves are entire, pinnately divided, often with stipules, sometimes with tendrils.

(33) Phlox / Polemoniaceae---herbaceous plants having flowers with 5 united sepals, 5 rounded united petals, 5 stamens and a 3-parted ovary. Leaves are entire and can be simple or pinnately divided.

(34) Pink / Caryophyllaceae---herbaceous plants with 5 se-pals, 5 rounded united petals, 10 stamens, and a 5-parted ovary. The entire, simple leaves are placed opposite on the stems which are swollen at the joints.

(35) Poppy / Papaveraceae---herbaceous plants having flowers with 2 deciduous sepals, 4 large petals, many stamens, and a large, many-seeded ovary. The leaves having petioles are mostly basal, hairy, and, pinnately divided.

(36) Primrose / Primulaceae---herbaceous plants with flowers having 5 sepals, 5 united petals, 5 stamens, and a 5-parted ovary. Leaves are mostly basal, and, usually, glabrous.

(37) Purslane / Portulacaceae---herbaceous plants with flowers having 2 sepals, 5 petals and usually 5 stamens that are connected to the petals. These are small plants with simple, smooth, entire, spatulate basal leaves.

(38) Rose / Rosaceae---plants or shrubs with flowers having 5 sepals, usually 5 petals, many stamens, and one to many fruits. Leaves are varied, but most have stipules.

(39) Sandlewood / Santalaceae---plants, sometimes parasitic, with 3 to 5 sepals and no petals. Leaves are usually simple and alternate, and often variegated.

(40) Saxifrage / Saxifragaceae---plants usually with mostly simple basal leaves and reduced, alternate stem leaves. Flowers have 5 sepals, 5 petals, 10 stamens, and a pronounced (often conc-shaped) ovary.

(41) Stonecrop, Sedum / Crassulaceae---small succulent plants with many thick, succulent, stalkless, undivided, stem leaves. Flowers have 4 or 5 sepals, 4 or 5 petals, and 8 or 10 stamens.

(42) Sundew / Droseraceae---small insectivorous plants, usually found in bogs. Leaves are sticky and mostly basal. Flowers have 5 sepals, 5 petals, and 5 stamens. These plants are not easily seen, so are not mentioned elsewhere in this book.

(43) Touch-me-not / Balsaminaceae---plants with thin, juicy leaves. Flowers have 3 petals and emerge from one large, bell-shaped sepal and 2 small ones. Seed pod pops open when touched.

(44) Valerian / Valerianaceae---plants with opposite stem leaves and petiolate basal leaves. Flowers have 5 joined petals and are bell-shaped or salverform.

(45) Violet / Violaceae---small plants with long-stemmed, heart-shaped leaves. Flowers are irregular, have 5 sepals, 5 petals, and a spur.

(46) Wintergreen / Pyrolaceae---small plants with simple, petiolate, evergreen leaves. Flowers are usually on a heavy stalk, often showing the color of the flowers. The flowers have 5 sepals, 5 somewhat waxy petals, 10 stamens, and a 5-parted ovary with a protruding style.

Corolla or flower parts

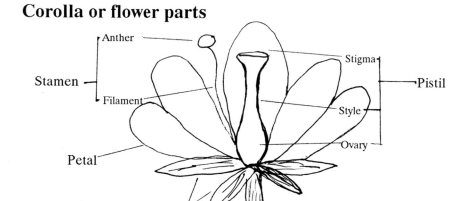

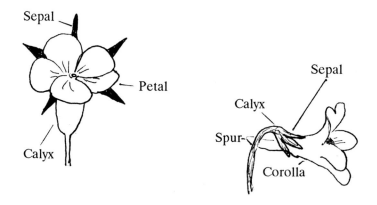

Pasque Flower (Denali Park)

Showing:

6 colorful purple sepals
Erect purplish pistil
Large cluster of yellow stamens
Long dense hairs on tips of sepals, and on new buds and leaves

COROLLA (FLOWER) TYPES

Regular or Symmetrical

Campanulate

Bell

Irregular

Funnel

Urn

Papilionaceous

Tube

Salverform

Labiate

Spurred

Spathe ———

Spadix ———

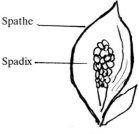

Floral-like Bract

INFLORESCENCES

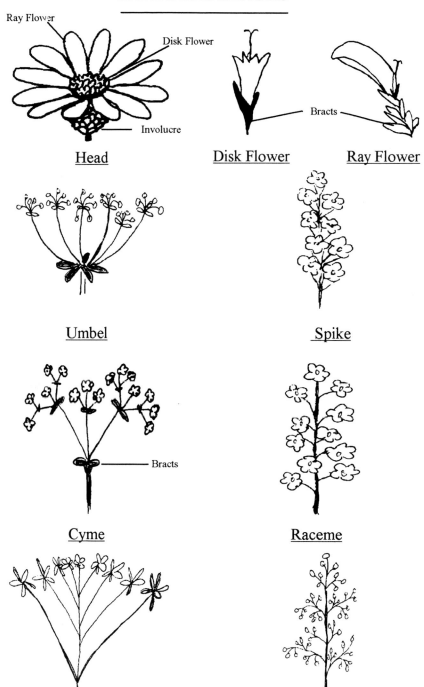

Head

Disk Flower

Ray Flower

Umbel

Spike

Cyme

Raceme

Corymb

Panicle

LEAF ARRANGEMENTS

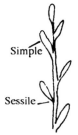

Simple

Sessile

Alternate

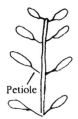

Petiole

Opposite

Palmate

Basal

Whorled

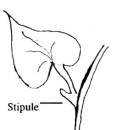

Stipule

Clasping

Lobed

Dissected

Pinnate

Compound Leaves

Sheathing

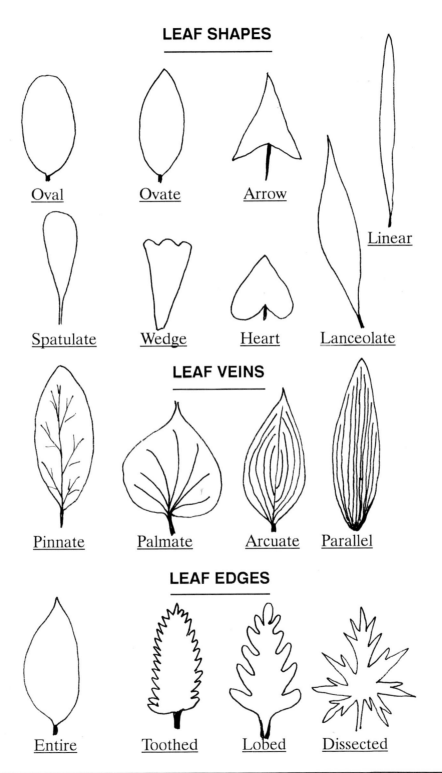

LEAF SHAPES

Oval Ovate Arrow Linear

Spatulate Wedge Heart Lanceolate

LEAF VEINS

Pinnate Palmate Arcuate Parallel

LEAF EDGES

Entire Toothed Lobed Dissected

OUTSTANDING AREAS

This section has been included to point out plants that are quite noticeable in specific areas along major highways. In many cases, they are too numerous to list. The following color code is used for convenience:

RR------Rose Red	Pur------Purple	R--------Red
P--------Pink	Y--------Yellow	Cr------Cream
Gr------Green	W--------White	Bl------Blue
Br------Brown	Lav------Lavender	O------Orange

Many trails are easily accessible, and, often, just a quick look around at a pulloff or lunch spot can be very rewarding. A good book on trails for hikes is "55 Ways to The Wilderness" by Helen Nienhueser and Nancy Simmerman, available at most bookstores.

ALASKA HIGHWAY (Whitehorse to Fairbanks)

1. Whitehorse to Haines Junction
Yukon Beardtongue---Pur/Bl
Beautiful Jacob's Ladder---Lav
Alpine Aster---W to P
Dwarf Fireweed---P
Fireweed---P
Wild Sweet Pea---P
Arctic Lupine---Bl
Alpine Milk Vetch---Lav & W
Death Camas---Cr
Stonecrop---Y
Siberian Aster---Lav
Lodgepole Pine
Senecio (Groundsel species)---Y

2. Destruction Bay
Round leaf Orchid---P
Northern White Ladies Slipper---W
Northern Green Bog Orchid---Gr
Bog Candle---W
Tundra Rose---Y
Alpine Milk Vetch---Lav & W
Dwarf Fireweed---P
Low-bush Cranberry---P to W

3. Tok to Fairbanks
Yellow Paintbrush---Y
Gentiana barbata---Bl
Pasque Flower---Pur
Siberian Aster---Lav
Few-flowered Shooting Star---P
Decumbent Goldenrod---Y
Wild Rhubarb---Cr
Cnidium cnidifolium---W
Death Camas---Cr
Fireweed---P
Jacob's Ladder---Lav

Tok to Fairbanks (cont'd)
Eskimo Potato---P
Wild Sweet Pea---P
Strawberry Spinach---R
Four-parted Gentian---Lav
Yarrow---W
Arctic Lupine---Bl
Tundra Rose---Y
Pink Pyrola---P
Large-flowered Wintergreen---W
Tall Wormwood
Larkspur---Bl
Soapberry
Coltsfoot---W or P
Grass of Parnassus---W
Bedstraw---W
Silverberry---Y
Pond Lily---Y
Yellow Dryas---Y

GEORGE PARKS HIGHWAY (Fairbanks to Palmer)

1. Fairbanks
Creamer's Field is a self-guided nature walk.   It is a very easy walk through fields and woods, with maps and signs on well marked trails. It is best in June and July.

2. Healy / Bison Gulch (Mile 243.5) area
Woods to alpine, moderate to difficult terrain, good late May through mid-July. Ridge to west side of highway at Bison Gulch is particularly interesting.
Tundra Rose---Y
Alpine Arnica---Y
Frigid Arnica---Y
Mountain Avens---W
Pasque Flower---Pur
Lapland Rosebay---P
Parry's Wallflower---P, W or Lav
Wild Sweet Pea---P
Eskimo Potato---P
Narcissus flowered Anemone---W
One-flowered Potentilla---Y
Lapland Diapensia---W
Purple Oxytrope---Pur
Yellow Oxytrope---Y
Splendid Oxytrope---P
Low Senecio species---Y
Mountain Forget-me-not---Bl
Wind Flower---W
Pink Plumes---P
Yellow Anemone---Y
Moss Gentian---Bl
White Pyrola---W
Elegant Paintbrush---P
Purple Mountain Saxifrage---Pur
Alaska Poppy---Y
Purple Cress---P, Pur or Lav

3. Denali National Park area (Mile 237)
> Similar to above, woods to alpine. Easy to difficult. Best in June & July

4. Mile 104-137 area
> Ostrich Fern in wet seepage

5. Mile 98.7, Talkeetna Turnoff, Mary Carey's famous Fiddlehead Fern (Ostrich Ferns)Farm & Gift Shop.

6. Mile 71, Junction of Hatcher Pass Road

TOK CUTOFF

> Tall Jacob's Ladder---Lav
> Dock---R
> Mastodon Flower---Y
> Dwarf Fireweed---P
> Patches of Orchids---W & P
> Yarrow---W
> Bluebells---Bl
> Pink Pyrola---P
> White Pyrola---W
> Tundra Rose---Y
> Fireweed---P
> Pussytoes---P & W

GLENN HIGHWAY (Glenallen to Anchorage)

1. Glenallen area, Junction of Richardson Highway
> Northern White Ladies Slipper---W
> Round-leaf Orchid---P&W
> Arctic Lupine---Bl
> Jacob's Ladder---Lav
> Siberian Aster---Lav
> Labrador Tea---W
> Wild Sweet Pea---P
> Eskimo Potato---P
> Yarrow---W
> Marsh Felswort---Bl
> Pink Pyrola---P
> Large-flowered Wintergreen---W
> Tundra Rose---Y

2. Sheep Mountain area
> Hairy Arctic Milk Vetch---Y
> Parry's Wallflower---P, W or Lav
> Narcissus-flowered Anemone---W
> Wind Flower---W
> Black Tipped Groundsel---Y
> Yellow Anemone---Y
> Pink Plumes---P
> Grass of Parnassus---W
> Labrador Tea---W
> Pink Pussytoes---P
> White Pussytoes---W
> Kinnikinnick---P
> Monkshood---Bl
> Blueberries---P
> Coltsfoot---W or P
> Forget-me-not---Bl
> Horizontal Juniper

Sheep Mt. area (cont'd)
Soap Berry
Pussytoes---W or P
Pink Pyrola---P
Large-flowered Wintergreen---W
Arctic Lupine---Bl
Northern Goldenrod---Y
Dogwood---W
Labrador Tea---W
Oxytropes---W or Y
Yellow Paintbrush---Y
Alaska Sage Brush

3. Matanuska Glacier Wayside
Woodland to alpine, easy to difficult terrain, best in early June.

4. Long Lake area
Bluebells---Bl
Soap Berry
White Pussytoes---W
Pink Pussytoes---P
Pink Pyrola---P
Large-flowered Wintergreen---W
Arctic Lupine---Bl
Northern Goldenrod---Y
Dogwood---W
Labrador Tea---W
White Oxytrope---W
Yellow Oxytrope---Y
Yellow Paintbrush---Y
Alaska Sage Brush
Golden Corydalis---Y

4. King Mt. Wayside
Fields , woods and glacial river, easy walking, much like Palmer area,June and July.

5. Hatcher Pass Road & Independence Mine State Park
Woodlands to alpine, easy to difficult terrain, good in mid-June to early August. Very wide variety of plant life.

6. Palmer area
Prickly Rose---P
Silverberry
Bluebells---Bl
Cow Parsnip---W
Wild Geranium---Lav
Wild Sweet Pea---P
Eskimo Potato---P
Nootka Lupine---Bl
Red Twig Dogwood---W
Yellow Oxytrope---Y
Calypso Orchid---P
Jacob's Ladder---Lav
Yellow Dryas---Y
Mustard Weed---Y
Rape---Y
Twinflower---W and P
Dogwood---W

Yellow Spotted Orchid---Y
Pink Pyrola---P
Large-flowered Wintergreen---W
Blue Columbine---Bl
Cut-leaf Anemone---Cr
Introduced Clovers---W or P
   including Sweet Clover---W or Y
         and Cow Vetch---Lav

7. Eklutna Flats area (Between Palmer and Anchorage)
Wild Sweet Pea---P
Dwarf Fireweed---P
Shooting Star---P
False Solomon's Seal---W
Silverberry---Y
Chocolate Lily---Br
Marsh Cinquefoil---Br
Poison Water Hemlock---W
Alaska Cotton---W
Marsh Marigold---Y
Bog Bean---W
Wild Iris---Pur
Yellow Dryas---Y
Prickly Rose---P
Silverweed---Y

8. Eagle River Visitor Center, Chugach State Park, Mile 10, Eagle River Loop Road
Woodlands, easy terrain, good June through August.

9. Arctic Valley Ski Area, Ft. Richardson Turnoff
Alpine, easy to difficult terrain, good June through August

RICHARDSON HIGHWAY (Fairbanks to Valdez)

1. Fairbanks to Paxson
Northern part similar to Fairbanks. Remainder like the Alaska Highway.
See Tok to Fairbanks, Section 3, under Alaska Highway section.

2. Paxson to Glenallen
See Glenallen area, Section 1, under Glenn Highway.
Diamond Willow is common in swampy or wet areas.

3. Copper Center
Jacob's Ladder---Lav
Decumbent Goldenrod---Y
Pasque Flower---Pur
Arnica---Y
Cut-leaf Anemone---Cr

4. Thompson Pass (Blueberry Lake)
A very rich, quite wet, alpine region. Some notable different varieties seen here are:
Caltha-leaf Avens---Y
Fringed Grass of Parnassus---W
Coast Saxifrage---W

5. Thompson Pass to Valdez (A steep decline sometimes called "The Switzerland of America)
> Some especially notable species in the area descending from the Pass to Valdez are:
>> False Hellebore---Gr
>> Goatsbeard---W
>> Western Columbine---R
>> Salmonberry---P
>> Cow Parsnip---W
>> Mountain Ash---W
>> Elderberry---W

6. Valdez
> Valdez is a very wet, coastal area with varied ecosystems supporting mostly woodland and coastal plants.
>> Arctic Daisy
>> Beach Pea
>> Wild Celery
>> Lovage
>> Tall Buttercup

SEWARD HIGHWAY (Anchorage to Seward)

This is a very interesting region with many established hiking areas, ranging in difficulty from easy to quite strenuous. Some are listed below. (Mileages are measured from Seward).

1. Glen Alps (Chugach State Park entrance, access from Seward Hwy. to O'Malley Road, Hillside Dr., to Upper Huffman & Toilsome Hill Dr.)
> Easy access to wide variety of alpine plants. Mountain Hemlocks are prominent here. Easy to difficult terrain. Good early-June to August.

2. Turnagain Arm
> This area includes a wide range of plants from coastal to alpine varieties; all growing here at very low elevation. There is very good trail access. Some plants frequently encountered here (other than those listed at McHugh Creek, below) are:
>> Rusty Menziesia---O
>> Yellow Monkeyflower---Y
>> Salmonberry---P
>> Early Blueberry---P or W
>> Tall Blueberry (Huckleberry)
>> Mt. Hemlock
>> Sitka Spruce
>> Coast Saxifrage---W

3. McHugh Creek Wayside
> Sea level to alpine, easy to difficult terrain, good from June to August
>> Baneberry---W
>> Elderberry---W
>> Mt. Ash---W
>> Goatsbeard---Cr
>> *Draba incerta*---Y
>> Mouse ear Chickweed---W
>> Red Currant---R
>> Trailing Black Currant---P
>> Dog Violet---Pur
>> Selkirk's Violet---Lav

McHugh Creek (cont'd)
    Kinnikinnick---P
    Jacob's Ladder---Lav
    Prickly Saxifrage---Cr
    Cut-leaf Fleabane---P
    False Solomon's Seal---W
    Chocolate Lily---Br
    Shooting Star---P
    Service Berry---W
    Alpine Heuchera---W
    Cut-leaf Anemone---Cr
    Western Columbine---R&Y
    Devil's Club---W
    Bluebells of Scotland---Lav
    Parsley Hemlock---W
    Potentilla villosa----Y

2. Falls Creek (Mile 107)
    Woodland to alpine, moderate to difficult terrain, good in June and July.

3. Bird Creek (Mile 102)
    Woodland to alpine, difficult terrain, good from late May through early July.

4. Mt. Alyeska (Mile 90) A world-famous ski resort
    Woodland to alpine, difficult terrain, good in June and July. Try taking the chair-lift up and walking down.   Notables are Salmonberry, Mountain Hemlock, Tall Blueberry, and Sitka Spruce.

5. Whittier (reached by train from Portage Station)
    Sea level to alpine, easy to difficult, good June through August
    Salmonberry---P
    Tall Blueberries---P
    Skunk Cabbage---Y
    Coast Saxifrage---W

6. Portage, Portage Glacier, and area (Mile 80)
    Glacial terrain, easy, good June through July
    Lupines---Bl
    Lovage---W
    Angelica---W
    Pale Pink Poppy---P

7. Turnagain Pass (Mile 68)
    Alpine meadows, easy terrain, good mid-June to mid-August
    A very wide variety of alpine meadow plants, including:
    Stream Violet---Y
    Chocolate Lily---Br
    Bog Candle---W
    Sitka Valerian---W
    False Hellebore---Gr
    Douglas Gentian---W
    Nootka Lupine---Bl
    Sitka Burnet---W
    Triangular-leaf Fleabane---Y
    Western Buttercup---Y
    Nagoonberry---P

8. Summit Lake (Mile 45)
>Sub-alpine to alpine area, difficult terrain, July
>Broad-petaled Gentian---Bl
>Forget-me-not---Bl

9. Junction of Sterling Highway (Mile 37), to Homer

10. Trail to Carter & Crescent Lakes (Mile 33)
>Rapid ascent from woodland to alpine, difficult terrain, good mid-June to early August.

11. Seward
>Similar to Whittier, some introduced species.

STERLING HIGHWAY (Junction of Seward Highway (Mile 37) to Homer

1. Junction to Anchor River
>Common woodland and field plants including:
>All Pyrolas
>Low-bush Cranberry---W
>Bog Cranberry---P
>Twinflower---W and P
>Dogwood
>Elegant Goldenrod---Y

2. Anchor River to Homer
>Alpine meadows appear as you near Homer.

3. Homer
>Common woodland and field plants. Lyme Grass and beach plants.
>Alpine meadows on the East End Road and Diamond Ridge Road.
>Lovage---W
>Angelica---W
>Lyme Grass---Gr
>Beach Fleabane---Y
>Beach Greens---W
>Oyster Leaf---Bl
>Arctic Daisy---W
>Beach Pea---P & Pur

DENALI HIGHWAY (Junction of Richardson Highway at Paxson, to junction of George Parks Highway at Cantwell, length 133 miles)

1. Round Tangle Lake (Mile 21.3)
>East (Paxson) end is mostly alpine and tundra. Easy to moderate terrain with a very wide variety of plants much like Eagle Summit and Bison Gulch. Good from late June to late-July.

2. Cantwell
>Western section is mostly river plains and tundra. Easy to moderate terrain. Good mid-June through July.

STEESE HIGHWAY (Fairbanks to Circle)

1. Pinnel Mountain (Mile 85)
Alpine area, easy to difficult terrain, good in June and July. See Eagle Summit, below.

2. Twelve Mile Summit (Mile 86)
Alpine area, easy to difficult terrain, good in June and July, see Eagle Summit, below.

3. Eagle Summit (Mile 108)
This is one of the choice alpine areas in the State accessible by road.
This is only a partial list of plants common to the area:
Coltsfoot---W or P
Wooly Lousewort---P
Capitate Lousewort---Y
Groundsel---Y
Mt. Avens---W
Narcissus-flowered Anemone---W
Windflower---W
Kitten Tails---Bl
Yellow Anemone---Y
Snow Buttercup---Y
Lapland Rosebay---P
Mountain Forget-me-not---Bl
Alp Lily---W
Parry's Wallflower---P-W-Lav
Purple Cress---Lav, Pur or P
Nagoonberry---P
Alpine Azalea---P
Lapland Diapensia---W
Blue Anemone---W and Bl

BLOOMING TIME CHARTS

The following pages contain general guidelines to normal blooming times of most common plants. It is arranged first by color to follow the text section of the book, and then by month. Very little except Willows bloom before mid-May. An especially early or late Spring can affect the blooming time greatly; sometimes by as much as two weeks. Late blooming times shown for particular plants are usually for higher elevations or more northern latitudes.

Skyline Drive above Homer, overlooking the Homer Spit and Kachemak Bay.
Cow Parsnip seed head, Elderberries, Fireweed and Sitka Spruce (in August).

Blooming Time Charts

PLANT	MAY	JUNE	JULY	AUGUST	
Alaska Blue Anemone	▬	▬			
Dog Violet	▬	▬			
Marsh Violet	▬	▬			
Selkirk's Violet	▬	▬			
Purple Mt. Saxifrage	▬	▬			
Low Jacob's Ladder	▬	▬			
Forget-me-not		▬	▬		
Purple Cress		▬			
Blue Bells		▬	▬		
Purple Oxytrope		▬			
Few-flowered Corydalis		▬			
Iris		▬			
Lupine		▬	▬		
Alaska Violet		▬	▬		
Alpine Milk Vetch		▬	▬		
Alpine Veronica		▬	▬		
Brook Lime		▬	▬		
Blue Columbine		▬	▬		
Campanula aurita		▬	▬		
Campanula uniflora		▬	▬		
Siberian Aster		▬	▬		
Tall Jacob's Ladder		▬	▬		
Wild Geranium		▬	▬		
Glaucous Gentian		▬	▬		
Yukon Beardstongue		▬	▬		
Larkspur		▬	▬		
Monkshood		▬	▬		
Gentiana barbata				▬	
Bluebells of Scotland			▬	▬	
Mt. Harebell			▬	▬	
Marsh Felswort			▬	▬	
Star Gentian			▬	▬	
Four-parted Gentian			▬	▬	
Oyster Leaf			▬		
				▬	

PLANT	MAY	JUNE	JULY	AUGUST
Blueberry	███	██		
Bog Rosemary	███	███		
Calypso Orchid	███	██		
Cut-leaf Fleabane	███	██		
Douglasia	███	█		
Bog Cranberry	██	███		
Beach Pea	██	██		
Lapland Rosebay	██	██		
Arctic Lousewort	██	███		
Wooly Lousewort	██	███		
Whorled Lousewort	██	███		
Pedicularis sudetica	██	███		
Pink Plumes		████	██	
Nagoonberry	█	████	█	
Alpine Azalea		█		
Pussy Toes		███		
Moss Campion		████		
Parry's Wallflower		████		
Primroses		████	█	
Roses		████	█	
Salmonberry		███	███	
Shooting Star		██		
Paintbrushes		███	█	
Twinflower		███	█	
Wild Sweet Pea		███	█	
Eskimo Potato		████	█	
Spring Beauty		████	██	
Pink Pyrola		████	██	
Pale Pink Poppy		███	██	
Viscid Oxytrope		████		
Rhododendron camtschaticum		███	█	
Fireweed		███	████	██
Dwarf Fireweed		███	████	█
Siberian Spring Beauty		█	███	
Round Leaf Orchid		███	███	
Coastal Fleabane			████	████
Pale Corydalis			████	█
Willow Herbs			████	█

Blooming Time Charts

PLANT	MAY	JUNE	JULY	AUGUST
Snow Buttercup	████	██		
Eschscholts Buttercup	████	████		
Draba incerta	████	██		
Groundsel	██	████		
Silverberry	██	███		
Marsh Marigold	██	██		
Yellow Anemone	█	██████		
Golden Corydalis	██	█████		
Yellow Oxytrope	██	████		
One-flowered Cinquefoil	█	██████		
Villous Cinquefoil	█	██████		
Alpine Arnica		████		
Frigid Arnica		████		
Northern Goldenrod		████		
Yellow Dryas		████		
Alaska Poppy		████		
Hulten's Poppy		█████		
Western Buttercup		██████		
Hooker's Cinquefoil		█████		
Hairy Arctic Milk Vetch		██████		
Lessing's Arnica		████		
Paintbrush		████████		
Silverweed		██████		
Stream Violet		██████		
Ross Avens		██████		
Caltha leaf Avens		██████		
Capitate Lousewort		██████		
Labrador Lousewort		████████		
Yellow Spotted Saxifrage		██████		
Bog Saxifrage			████████	
Meadow Arnica			████████	
Black-tipped Groundsel			██████	
Marsh Fleabane (Mastodon Fl)			██████	
Tall Buttercup varieties			█████	
Shrubby Cinquefoil			█████	
Norwegian Cinquefoil			█████	
Solidago decumbens			█████	
Elegant Goldenrod			█████	
Monkey Flower			█████	
Pond Lily			█████	
Yellow Mt. Heather			█████	
Rattlebox			█████	
Large leaf Avens			█████	
Butter & Eggs			████████	

PLANT	MAY	JUNE	JULY	AUGUST
Yellow Willow Herb			███████	███
Beach Fleabane			███████	████
Triangular leaf Fleabane			███████	█████

* *

WHITE AND CREAM-COLORED FLOWERS

PLANT	MAY	JUNE	JULY	AUGUST
Baneberry	████	██		
Serviceberry	████	██		
Bearberry	████	██		
Kinnikinnick	████	██		
Rock Cress	███	█████	█	
Wood Violet	███	███		
Leather Leaf	███	██		
Windflower		█████	█	
Cut leaf Anemone		███		
Parry's Wallflower		█████	█	
Prickly Saxifrage		███		
Grove Sandwort		███		
Coltsfoot		███		
Buckbean		█████		
Mt. Marigold		█████		
Mouse ear Chickweed		████		
Pussy Toes		████	█	
Cloudberry		████	█	
High-bush Cranberry		█████	█	
Low-bush Cranberry		███	██	
Bog Candle		███	██	
Hooded Ladies Tresses		███	██	
Red Twig Dogwood		███	██	
Diapensia		██████	██	
Arctic Sandwort		███	██	
Capitate Valerian		██	████	██
Bulblet Saxifrage		██	████	
Coast Saxifrage		██	███	
Brook Saxifrage		██	███	
Red-stemmed Saxifrage		██	███	
Trailing Raspberry		██	███	
Narcissus-flowered Anemone		███	██	
Mt. Avens		████	█	
Mt. Ash		████	█	
Elderberry		████	█	
Moss Heather		████	█	
Cat's Paw		████	██	
Bell Heather		███	██	

Blooming Time Charts

PLANT	MAY	JUNE	JULY	AUGUST	
False Solomon's Seal		▬▬▬▬			
Labrador Tea		▬▬▬			
Watermelon Berry		▬▬▬▬▬			
Sitka Valerian		▬▬▬▬▬			
Northern White Lady Slipper		▬▬▬▬			
Alaska Spirea		▬▬▬			
Single Delight		▬▬▬▬			
Large-flowered Wintergreen		▬▬▬▬			
Alpine Meadow Bistort		▬▬▬▬▬▬			
Bedstraw		▬▬▬▬			
Whitish Gentian		▬▬▬▬▬▬			
Death Camas		▬▬▬▬▬			
Alp Lily		▬▬▬			
Bunchberry		▬▬▬▬▬			
Tall Chickweed		▬▬▬▬▬			
Parsley Hemlock		▬▬▬▬▬			
Strawberry		▬▬			
Goatsbeard		▬▬▬▬▬▬			
Wild Rhubarb		▬▬			
Poison Water Hemlock			▬▬		
Willow Herbs			▬▬▬▬		
Alpine Heuchera			▬▬▬		
Alpine Spirea			▬▬▬▬▬		
Dwarf Water Lily			▬▬▬▬▬▬		
Grass of Parnassus			▬▬▬▬▬▬		
Sitka Burnet			▬▬▬▬▬		
Wild Calla			▬▬▬▬▬		
Wild Camomile			▬▬▬▬▬		
Wild Celery			▬▬▬▬		
Cow Parsnip			▬▬▬▬▬		
Lovage			▬▬▬▬		
Yarrow			▬▬▬▬▬▬▬		
Miscellaneous Plants					
Currants	▬▬▬▬				
Gooseberry	▬▬▬				
Timberberry	▬▬▬				
Crowberry	▬▬▬				
Frog Orchid		▬▬▬▬▬			
Yellow Spotted Orchid		▬▬▬▬▬			
Western Columbine		▬▬▬▬▬			
Prairie Sagewort		▬▬▬▬▬▬			

PLANT	MAY	JUNE	JULY	AUGUST
Arctic Wormwood		███████		
Chocolate Lily		███████		
Cotton Grass		████████████		
Devil's Club		████████		
Roseroot		███████		
Sidebells Pyrola		███████		
Artemisia Tilesii		████████		
Marsh Cinquefoil			██████	
Mt. Sorrel			██████	
Dock			████████	
Hellebore			██████████	
Rusty Menziesia		████████		
Broom Rape		████████		
Northern Green Bog Orchid		███████		
Pineapple Weed			██████████	

ALASKAN EDIBLES

(See keys to Type, Part Used, Preparation Method, and Use at end of listing)

Name	Type	Part	Prep	Use
Beach Greens	P	L,St	R,C	V
Bearberry	S	B	R,C	J
Bedstraw	P	Sd	D,R	D
Birch	T	F,St,L,S	R,C,D	V,G
Bistort	P	L	R,C	V
Bluebell	P	L	R,C	V
Blueberries	S	B	R,C	D,J,Fr
Bull Rush	P	Sh,R	R,C	V
Cattail	P	F,S,St	R,C	V
Celery, Wild	P	L,R,St	R,C	V,S
Chickweed	P	L,St	R,C	V
Chives	P	L,R	R,C	V,S
Cloudberry	S	B	R,C	D,J,Fr
Clover	P	F,L,St,R	C	D
Coltsfoot	P	L	C,D	V,S
Cottonwood	T	Bud	C	V
Cow Parsnip	P	St,R	R,C	V
Crabapple, Oregon	T	Fr	C	J
Cranberry, Bog	S	B	R,C	D,J
Cranberry, High-bush	S	B	R,C	D,J
Cranberry, Low-bush	S	B	R,C	D,J
Cresses	P	L,St	R.C	V
Crowberry	S	B	R,C	L,Fr
Currants	S	B	R,C	J
Dandelion	P	L,F,R	R,C,D	V,D
Devil's Club	S	St*2	R,C	M
Dock	P	L,St	R,C	V
Elderberry, Red	S	B*3,F	C	V,J
Eskimo Potato	P	R	C	V
Fern species	P	R,St *1	R,C	V
Fireweed	P	St,L,F	R,C	V,J
Glasswort	P	St	R	V
Gooseberry	S	B	R,C	D,J,Fr
Great Burnet	P	L	R,C	V
Hemlock	T	L	C	D

Name	Type	Part	Prep	Use
Huckleberry	S	B	R,C	D,J,Fr
Jewel Weed	P	L,St	R,C	V
Juniper, Common	S	Fr	D	S
Kinnikinnick	S	B	C	J
Labrador Tea	S	L	C	D
Lamb's Quarters	P	L,St	R,C	V
Lily, Chocolate	P	R,Sd	R,C	V
Lily, Pond	P	R,Sd	C,D	G
Lousewort	P	R	C	V
Mare's Tail	P	St	C	V
Marigold, Marsh	P	L*3,St*3	C	V
Monkey Flower	P	L,St	R,C	V
Mountain Ash	T	B	C	Fr
Mustard Weed	P	L,St	R,C,D	V,S
Nagoonberry	S	B	R,C	D,J,Fr
Nettle	P	L,St	C	V
Orchid, Calypso	P	R	R	V
Parry's Wallflower	P	L,R	R,C	V
Pineapple Weed	P	F	C	D
Plantain	P	L	R	V,M
Raspberry	S	B,L	R,C,D	D,J,Fr
Raspberry, Trailing	S	B	R,C	D,J,Fr
Rhubarb, Wild	P	R	R,C	V,M
Rose	S	F,L,Fr*4	R,C,D	J,Fr,D
Rosewort	P	L,St,R	R,C	V
Salal	S	B	R,C	J
Salmonberry	S	B	R,C	D,J,Fr
Saxifrage, Brook	P	L	R,C	V
Saxifrage, Red-stemmed	P	L	R,C	V
Scurvy Grass	P	L	R,C	V
Serviceberry	S	B	R,C,D	J,Fr
Silverberry	S	B	C	V
Silverweed	P	R	C	V
Soapberry	S	B	R	Fr
Sorrel	P	L,St	R,C	V
Spring Beauty	P	R,St,L	R,C	V
Spruce	T	L,S	C	D
Strawberry	P	B,L	R,C,D	D,J,Fr
Strawberry Spinach	P	L,St,F	R,C	V,J
Sundew	P	L	R	V
Sweet Gale	S	L	D	S
Thimbleberry	S	B	R,C	D,J,Fr
Timberberry	P	B	R	Fr

Name	Type	Part	Prep	Use
Violet	P	L,St,F	R,C	V
Water Smartweed	P	R	C	V
Watermelon Berry	P	B,L,St	R,C	V,J,D
Willows	S,T	L,St,F	R,C	M,V
Willows, Dwarf	S	R	R,C	V
Wormwood	P	L	R,C	S
Yarrow	P	St,L	C	S,D

KEYS:

Plant Type	Part Used	Preparation	Use
S---Shrub	R---Root	R---Raw	V---vegetable
P---Plant	St---Stem	C---Cooked	G---Grain
T---Tree	L---Leaf	D---Dried	D---Drink
	S---Sap		J---Jellies
	F---Flower		S---Seasoning
	B---Berry		P---Pickles
	Sd---Seed		Fr---Fruit
	Fr---Fruit		M---Medicinal
	Sh---Shoots		

SPECIAL ATTENTION:

*1-----Use with caution
*2-----Underground Stem
*3-----Contains poison that is broken down by boiling
*4-----Spit out seeds

POISONOUS PLANTS

MARSH MARIGOLD *(Caltha jpalustris)*---Pioson is broken down by boiling.

ALL ANEMONES *(Anemone species)*---All contain poisonous anemonin.

BUTTERCUP *(Ranunculus species)*---For emergency food use, poison can be broken down by boiling and changing water.

BANEBERRY *(Actaea rubra)*---Both red and white-berried plants very poisonous. Six berries have been known to kill a small child.

MONKSHOOD *(Aconitum species)*---All parts Poisonous. Once called Wolfbane.

LARKSPUR *(Delphinium species)*---Poisonous like Monkshood, but not quite as active.

FALSE HELLEBORE *(Veratrum viride)*---Very Poisonous. Extremely bitter. Death results from respiratory depression and asphyxia.

DEATH CAMAS *(Zygadenus elegans)*---Same as above.

BLUE FLAG *(Iris setosa)*---Irritant substance in leaves. Non-flowering plant mistaken for Cattail. Rhizome poisonous. Powdered rhizome called "Orris Root" formerly used in cosmetics; it is EXTREMELY allergenic!

WILD SWEET PEA *(Hedysarum Mackenzii)*---Edibility very questionable.

LUPINE *(Lupinus species)*---Leaves and seeds poisonous.

WATER HEMLOCK *(Cicuta Mackenzieana & Cicuta Douglasii)*---Considered by many authorities to be the most virulent poisonous plant in the North Temperate Zone. Death has been known to occur within 20 minutes of ingestion.

ELDERBERRY *(Sambucus racemosa)*---All parts poisonous. The pulp of berries is the least toxic part of plant. Uncooked berries may produce nausea if too many are eaten. Cooking should break down the toxins.

LABRADOR TEA *(Ledum palustre)*---Reports of cathartic effect if too much tea is consumed. The robustly aromatic leaves make it one of the most famous teas in the North Country.

FALSE LILY OF THE VALLEY *(Maianthemun dilatatum)*---Contains cardiac glycosides (alkaloids).

FIR CLUB MOSS *(Lycopodium selago)*---Contains a poisonous alkaloid causing pain in mouth, vomiting and diarrhea.

WILD CALLA *(Calla palustris)*---Entire plant, especially berries, contains poisonous acids and burning saponin-like substances, neutralized by drying or boiling.

DEVIL'S CLUB *(Echinopanax horridum)*---Berries contain a toxin and are considered inedible.

BOG ROSEMARY *(Andromeda polifolia)*---Contains Andromedotoxin---causes lowered blood pressure, difficult breathing, vomiting, diarrhea and cramps.

IMPORTANT NOTES:

Remember, it takes less poison to be fatal to a small child than for an adult.

Impress upon your family and friends to never eat any unknown plant or berry.

In case of poisoning, contact medical personnel and be prepared to tell them the name of the plant involved. Better to be safe, even if embarrassed, than dead. Save evidence which might help identify the plant.

GLOSSARY OF BOTANICAL TERMS

Acute: Sharply pointed.

Alpine: Growing above timberline.

Alternate: Leaf or branch arrangement on stem, not opposite each other.

Annual: A plant growing from seed, blooming, setting seed and then dying all in one growing season.

Arcuate: Usually referring to veins in a leaf; bowed or following a curve looking nearly parallel.

Basal: Situated at, or pertaining to, the base.

Berry: A soft, fleshy, multi-seeded fruit.

Bi-pinnately divided: Describing a pinnate leaf in which the leaflets are further divided in a pinnate fashion.

Biennial: Of two seasons' duration from seed to maturity and death.

Binomial: The botanical nomenclature, or scientific name of a plant; consisting of the genus name and the species name.

Bloom: A whitish coating on a fruit that, usually, can be rubbed off.

Bog: A low, very wet area. Soil is often acidic, and standing water is common.

Bract: A reduced or modified leaf, usually below a flower. Often petal-like.

Bristles: Long, stiff hairs.

Calyx: The outermost circle of the floral parts. The external portion, usually green. The group of sepals.

Campanulate: Bell-shaped.

Capitate: Having a dense, head-like cluster.

Capsule: A dry fruit composed of more that 1 seed cavity.

Catkin: A tight spike of petalless flowers (usually either male or female).

Clasping: Partially surrounding the stem (usually referring to a leaf petiole).

Cluster: A tight grouping, or bunch.

Cyme: A flat-topped flower cluster, with central flowers opening first.

Deciduous: Not persistent, said of leaves falling in Autumn or of floral parts falling after flowering.

Dentate: Having a margin or edge cut with sharp teeth directed outward.

Entire: Without divisions, lobes, or teeth. With even or smooth margin or edge.

Ethnic: Pertaining to a person, or group of people, who are native to, or have traditionally lived in, an area.

Evergreen: Remaining green all year.

Fall: A term for the large, petal-like sepals of the Iris family.

Frond: Leaf of a fern. (Also, a large leaf).

Genus: A group of closely related plants. The first part of a binomial or scientific name.

Glabrous: Having a smooth, even surface without hairs.

Glaucous: Having a waxy, grayish-blue appearance.

Heath: Open wasteland, with usually acidic soil.

Herbaceous: A non-wood, perennial plant, with above ground parts dying to the ground each year.

Hummock: A rounded rise of vegetation Usually in a wet area; such as, a bog or marsh.

Hybrid: A cross between 2 species or subspecies, usually of the same genus.

Incisions: Sharp cuts or indentations, usually referring to leaf edges.

Inflorescence: A flower cluster, or grouping on a stem.

Insectivorous: Referring to plants that capture insects; and absorb nutriment from them.

Introduced: Said of plants that were not originally native to an area. Becoming established after escaping from farmlands or in reseeding projects.

Involucre: A group of bracts beneath a flower cluster, as in the heads of the Aster Family.

Lanceolate: Narrow, tapering to both ends.

Leaflet: A single part of a compound leaf.

Lobed: Describing a leaf that is divided into curved or rounded parts connected to each other by an undivided central area.

Meadow: A moist, open area, usually free of shrubs and trees.

Node: A joint in a stem, or the point on a stem where the leaf starts.

Oblanceolate: Similar to lanceolate, but broader at base.

Oblong: Much longer than broad, with nearly parallel margins and a rounded tip.

Opaque: Not letting light through, not transparent nor translucent.

Ovary: The lower swollen portion of the reproductive part of a plant, containing the seeds.

Palmate: Lobed, divided or ribbed so as to resemble the outstretched fingers of a hand.

Parasitic: An organism obtaining food and/or shelter at the expense of another.

Pedicel: The stalk attaching individual flowers to the main stem of the inflorescence.

Perennial: Living for more than two years; and, usually, flowering each year after the first.

Petal: Usually the colorful part of the corolla, usually colored.

Petiolate: Having a petiole.

Petiole: The stalk that attaches the leaf to the stem.

Pinnate: Describing a compound leaf in which the leaflets are arranged in two rows, one on each side of the midrib.

Pistil: A term used ambiguously to describe either a single carpel (simple pistil) or a group of fused carpels (compound pistil).

Pistillate: A flower that has only the female reproductive parts.

Prickle: A short woody pointed outgrowth from the epidermis of a plant.

Raceme: An inflorescence in which the flowers are formed on individual pedicels attached to the main stem.

Ray Flower: The flat outer flowers of the Aster family, often incorrectly referred to as petals of a Daisy.

Reflexed: Bent abruptly downward or backward.

Revegetate: To plant again. Usually an attempt to restore to original or acceptable condition.

Rhizome: An underground stem or rootstalk, usually rooting at the nodes, becoming upcurved at the end.

Rosette: A crowded cluster of leaves, appearing to rise from one point in the ground.

Salverform: A tube-shaped flower, with petals that flatten out at right angles from the tube.

Sepal: One of the outer group of floral parts. Usually green .

Serrated: Having sharply pointed teeth or indentations.

Sessile: Without a stalk or stem.

Sheath: A tubular (often thin) plant structure that surrounds a plant part. Often at a connection where petiole meets stem. Typical of many members of the Parsley. family.

Shrub: A woody perennial, smaller than a tree, usually with several basal stems.

Silicle: The seed capsule of some members of the Mustard family, usually no more than twice as long as wide.

Silique: The seed capsule of many members of the Mustard family, more than twice as long as wide.

Spadix: A thick fleshy stem (like a spike) that bears many flowers and fruits of a plants.

Spathe: A large bract, or pair of bracts, often petal-like, enclosing a flower cluster or spadix.

Spatulate: Describing structures that have a broad end and a long narrow base, such as the leaves of the Daisy.

Species: A further division of plants beyond genus, showing slight differences. More specifically, the specific epithet, or second part of the binomial or scientific name.

Spike: An inflorescence like a raceme, but without individual flower stems.

Spore: The small, dust-like, asexual, unicellular reproductive body of flowerless plants.

Spur: A tubular or sac-like part of a flower. It usually contains a nectar secreting gland.

Stamen: The male organ of the flower, consisting of a filament and an anther, the latter bearing the pollen.

Staminate: A flower that has only the male reproductive parts.

Stellate: Star-shaped.

Stigma: The top part of a pistil or style, often hairy and/or sticky, which receives the pollen at pollination time and on which the pollen grain germinates.

Stipe: The stalk beneath the ovary. The leaf stalk of a fern.

Stipule: A part of the leaf where it attaches to the stem (especially common in the Rose and Pea families). A broadening on either side of the stem that could be mistaken for a bract.

Stomata (singular stoma): Small openings or pores in the surface of a leaf through which gaseous exchange takes place between the internal tissues and the atmosphere.

Style: The tubular part of the reproductive portion of a plant that connects the stigma to the ovary.

Succulent: Fleshy, juicy.

Tendril: A long thread-like part of a plant stem that supports it by twining around other objects. Notable in members of the Pea family.

Terminal: At the end.

Tubular: Having the form of, or consisting of, a tube or tubes.

Tundra: Treeless Arctic plain, often times damp and having mounds.

Umbel: An inflorescence, more or less flat-topped, in which all of the pedicels arise at the same point, like the ribs of an umbrella.

Waste Places: Areas where soil has been stripped of its naturally occurring vegetation. Usually lack of humus, soil and care causes it to develop into a different environment and plant community than it was originally. Generally referring to roadside pull-offs, old roadbeds, around old buildings and townsites.

Watery: Juicy. Said of plants with a non-fibrous stem.

Whorl: An arrangement of leaves, etc., in a circle around the stem, radiating from a node. Three or more leaves or flowers at one node, in a circle.

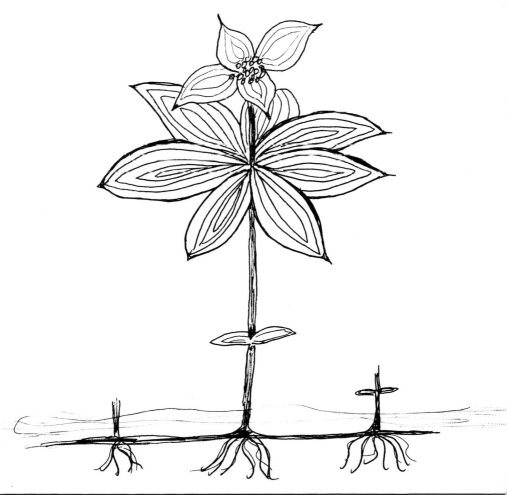

BIBLIOGRAPHY

Graham, Frances K. 1985. *Plant Lore of an Alaskan Island.* Alaska Northwest Publishing Company, Anchorage, Alaska. 194 pp.

Heller, Christine. *1953. Wild Edible and Poisonous Plants of Alaska.* Univ. Alaska Ext. Bull. F-40. 87 pp.

_____. 1966. *Wildflowers of Alaska.* Graphics Arts Center, Portland, Oregon. 103 pp.

Hultén, Eric. 1968. *Flora of Alaska and Neighboring Territories.* Stanford University Press. 1008 pp.

Kari, Priscilla R. *1987. Tanaina Plantlore. Dena'ina K'et'una.* National Park Service, Alaska Region. 205 pp.

Nienhueser, Helen, and Simmerman, Nancy, 1981, *55 Ways to the Wilderness in Southcentral Alaska*, The Mountaineers, Seattle, Washington. 166 pp.

Smith, James P., Jr. 1977. *Vascular Plant Families.* Mad River Press, Eureka, California. 321 pp.

Viereck, Leslie A. , and Little, Elbert L., Jr. *1972. Alaska Trees and Shrubs*. Forest Service, U.S. Dept. of Agriculture. Washington, D.C. 266 pp.

Welsh, Stanley L. 1974. *Anderson's Flora of Alaska and Adjacent Parts of Canada.* Brigham Young University Press, Provo, Utah. 724 pp.

INDEX

Page numbers in **bold type** indicate color photographs.